Christ and Reason

Christ and Reason
An Introduction to Ideas from Kant to Tyrrell

GEORGE WILLIAM RUTLER

Christendom Press

TO THE MEMORY OF

CUTHBERT AIKMAN SIMPSON

Regius Professor of Hebrew

and

Dean of Christ Church

OXFORD

... the Roman Church, *tam antiqua et tam nova*,
haunted by many recurring conflicts and crises,
skilled in statesmanship, enriched by
unfathomable memory, is a vigilant
Mother-Confessor and a wise Director of Souls.
A candid Protestant, or an honest humanist
will find himself at least asking — what in a
world rocking in helpless indecision and
revealing ominous cracks of threatened collapse,
will become of our Christian heritage and
traditional culture should that Church
compromise its sense of divine commission or,
if bribed or tortured by lust of power, it
should tremble to impose its own discipline,
lose its nerve and snap under the breaking strain?

J. M. Lloyd Thomas
The Hibbert Journal (1951)

Table of Contents

Preface

A couple of newspapers recently took the Pope to task for saying in public audience that the sacrifice of Christ has superseded the sacrifice of bulls and goats. Anyone who takes theology seriously could be heartened by this concern of secular editors. From a more pedestrian viewpoint, it would appear that they are interested in the subject because religious attitudes have momentary political significance for a host of international issues from the Middle East to Eastern Europe. The newspapers would hardly otherwise direct their editorial columns to what the Epistle to the Hebrews says about the treatment of animals in Solomon's Temple.

Particularly revealing is the assumption that so radical a theological doctrine can only be a matter of opinion, and that the Pope is arbitrary for making a point of it. It is as though any theological statement is more revealing psychologically than analytically, and what makes the theological opinion of a public figure important is that someone who is important talks deliberately about something which intelligent people should consider unimportant. Now this kind of attitude is the result of a modern unwinding by which statements about eternal truths have been divorced from reason; then there are no eternal truths, and faith is like a gas bubbling up from the surface of reality, a subjective disposition instead of an objective virtue. Theology has been removed gradually from its place in rational science and made rather to substitute poetically where science is incomplete. From the time Immanuel Kant removed revealed truths from the access of reason, suspicions about the theological virtues hardened into tenets: faith is self-projection, hope is optimism, and love is sentiment.

Any of these notions can become plausible once supernatural reality is thought to be unnatural. The classical theologians of the Church labored to understand how nature stands in relation to things supernatural and is perfected by grace. Only such an enterprise can venture to say as did the Second Vatican Council: "Far from thinking that works produced by man's own talent and energy are in opposition to God's power, and that the rational creature exists as a kind of rival to the Creator, Christians are convinced that the triumphs of the human race are a sign of God's grace and the flowering of His own mysterious design." (*Gaudium et Spes*, n. 34) The same Council, not toppling from the summit of hope into the clouds of optimism, said that man has become a question to himself. (ibid., n. 21) This questioning is not the philosopher's perennial inquiry into the abode of light; it has become a sinister confrontation with the self in the form of anxiety. Man becomes hollow when he becomes anthropocentric, and when he sees nothing but himself he finds nothing in himself. The human fact is the creation of God, and the fact remains anxious so long as the divine Logos, the constituent of all meaning, is treated as a peripheral question instead of an intrinsic exclamation.

At the present stage in the denouement of bias against God, the observer confronts competing images: an unexpected and dramatic repudiation of atheistic dialecticism in Marxist social orders, and a sleepy rejection of theism as a practical moral reality in the West. As the only predictable thing about the unpredictable is that it can happen, rash would be the critic who thinks that either trend will condition the culture which is now about to replace the intuitions of the twentieth century. One thing is certain, however. The highly tenuous Modernist complaint against Catholicism has declined from what erudition it might once have mustered. Theology is at an inferior level today, and the popularization of old heresies is even worse.

The student beginning theology is at a particular disadvantage for having been deprived of an historical perspective. This is a neglect of recent educational policies, and it has taken its toll. What appears to make sense in recent Modernist exercises only does so when the audience is unaware of the various thinkers who said much the same in times past, but said it better, furnishing their arguments from a store of scholarship superior to present theology. Of the figures glanced at in the following chapters, perhaps only Tyrrell submitted inadequate scholarship to inadequate character. Much can be learned from them, or of them, in any case. Even more can one benefit from those scholars who in their own day represented the truth against some of the same challenges now posed by less eloquent voices. Cardinal Newman will be a protagonist where he is mentioned in the following pages. Like Cicero who would rather be wrong with Plato than right with the Pythagoreans, one would not be the poorer for being wrong with Newman, although there are high odds from a high place in Newman's favor.

As the following are essays, they can only introduce some names and books which may be unfamiliar to the Catholic reader but which, once met, may help to develop more discrimination in judging some of the vagaries which pass for substance in lecture rooms. A small collection can touch on a few figures and usually one representative book by each: Kant's *Religion Within the Limits of Reason Alone*, Kierkegaard's *Philosophical Fragments*, Newman's *An Essay in Aid of a Grammar of Assent*, Kähler's *The So-Called Historical Jesus and the Historic, Biblical Christ*, Harnack's *What is Christianity?*, Tyrrell's *Christianity at the Cross-Roads*. The works of others should be given place in a larger study; but these are presented as vignettes, not uncritical in opinion, with the idea at least of indicating an interesting path by which the influence of Immanuel Kant has affected the health of logic in the deepest attentions of the mind.

Kant on the Limits of Reason

The Difficulty of Judgments Outlined

At the age of seventy, when he might have retired to reflect upon an ordered if constrained life, Immanuel Kant (1724-1804) pointed his quill at a puzzle he had faced a dozen years earlier in the *Critique of Pure Reason*. The whole burden of the *Critique* in one sense had been the heart of all metaphysical problems: the possibility of knowing something that, though not contained in "the notion of a subject," is known prior to and independent of experience. Such knowledge would be a product of what he called "synthetic *a priori* judgment."

Now judgments of this sort abound in physics and mathematics, as the *Critique* explains, and all metaphysical judgments are of that order. The high metaphysical questions about God, free will, and immortality are known *a priori*; and they do not lend themselves to empirical sense. So then, any possibility of making judgments about them depends on a "transcendental" use of pure reason. "Transcendental," as Kant means it here, is not above finite being. It only means the apprehension of a truth which is not based on experience: "I apply the term transcendental to all knowledge which is not so much occupied with objects as with the mode of our cognition of these objects, so far as this mode is possible *a priori*."[1] Kant's whole effort reaches its height when he considers the ways of God to man. Possibly the definitive method of Kant is outlined in

---

[1]Immanuel Kant, *Critique of Pure Reason* (London: 1969), p. vii, hereafter *CPR*. Cf. Eric Mascall, *Existence and Analogy* (London: 1967), p. 99n.

the magisterial Preface to the first edition of *Religion Within the Limits of Reason Alone*.[2]   He considers why, as he claims, "morality leads inevitably to religion"; this he regards as a synthetic *a priori* proposition. And in so doing he launches the problematic adventure of method which for good and ill has engaged spirits kindred and alien alike right to our own day.

From the start of his project, a deep chasm quite obviously exists between Kant's philosophy and any type of philosophical realism. St. Thomas, with Aristotle, held that nothing is in the human intellect unless it first is in the senses. In other words, all human knowledge begins with sense experience. Two difficulties then follow from an assertion of morality leading inevitably to religion. For the realist, knowledge of even such general terms as "morality" and "religion" begins from particular experiences, and is therefore not, in the profoundest degree, *a priori*. Secondly, Kant's practical agnosticism prevents him from appreciating how, in the Scholastic tradition, religion is a moral virtue related to justice. His understanding of the two terms "morality" and "religion" is thus far from the classical Christian view.

The distinction from Christianity becomes an affinity for some present-day attitudes.   There certainly is some sleek parallel between Kant opening his grand discourse in the fullness of his years, and the mixed confidences of thinkers at the end of the twentieth century. Kant claimed belief in God, and he also believed the prouder protests of the Enlightenment; he casts a sympathetic shadow on the particular intellect who in our late times retains a theism not unscarred by the contests of modern materialism.   Whether the remaining belief was a faithful remnant is disputable, and conditions much of the contemporary difficulty with religious thought and speech. While nothing in fact can be "post-Christian" since Christ is the Omega, and thus has no sequel, popular culture can decline from Christian

---

[2]Immanuel Kant, *Religion Within the Limits of Reason Alone*, trans. Green and Hudson (New York: 1960), hereafter *RWLRA*.

culture. Kant was "post-Christian," in the cultural sense, to the extent that his social formation had known and renounced some venerable religious assumptions. Like someone growing up in the remaining days of popular American religiosity, Kant had been formed by the pietistic school of Philip Jakob Spener (1635-1705) during his early studies in the Collegium Fredericianum from 1732 to 1740. But also like someone who had struggled through the social unrest and scepticism of post-Eisenhower America, Kant had met the heady enticements of the Wolffian rationalism which was defining the curriculum in the University of Konigsburg where he matriculated in 1740, and where he became the rough equivalent of a Fellow in 1754.

The mental cauldron inevitably yielded a mixture of sympathies and aversions which in some measure shape the substance of theological method in our generation, not loath to call itself both post-Christian and post-Modern. A mind intense as Kant's saw the tension in trying to account for divine omniscience and human autonomy. It was too anxious for the old verities which sought resolution in the panoply of mystery; to him that seemed more like a magician's cloak of deceit. Yet it was too acute to settle for the efficient kind of debunking offered by the rationalism of Leibniz or the sceptical empiricism of Hume. He was willing to say that there is horizon beyond the horizon, but how to explain it was another matter.

He venerated what he thought to be the historical Jesus whose ethic he distinguished from traditional Christianity. His vision of Jesus as a metaphysical fact was moral to the exclusion of eschatology; that is to say, Christ looms as a guide to the virtuous life rather than as the medium of eternal bliss wrought by salvation from sin. The reader quickly enough gets the impression of an author embarking on one last effort to describe a grand system of religious associations and tendencies which might salvage the essence of religion as he had kept it in youth, and who confounds his own protestations by creating a wholly other system with each flourish of mind and pen.

He does not write as a theologian; but he does write to theologians. If some accounts are to believed, the philosopher made recourse to a catechism from his childhood to brush off the cobwebs on his store of doctrinal terms. A dangerous archeologism it was, giving the false impression that he knew the meaning of the Christian vocabulary entire, and particularly that he knew what Christianity means by grace and atonement. The earnest restoration yielded only a stage set, a scenery of primitive Christian vistas but not the scene itself. This was not the first instance of overwrought competence. Forty years earlier in the *Universal Natural History and Theory of the Heavens* he claimed a cosmogonical competence greater than Newton's, apparently without having ever read the *Principia*.[3]

"A poor bungler" by his own admission at least in comparison to "Christ's work," Kant's professed intention was to amplify the moral consequences of given dogma. The result was quite other. There appeared in fact the technical furniture for a new ethical system, largely innocent of recent Biblical scholarship, censorious of the emotionalism which to him was a mark of pietist hypocrisy, and nonetheless deeply complected by the inheritance of the same old outlook. Such pietism, which had a Catholic cousin in Jansenism, became known in colonial North America through sects like the Mennonites, Amish and Methodists. It preached a rigid rejection of rigid dogmatism, enthused by the heady power of individualism which seemed as limitless as the new land, and scornful of the hierarchical constitution of the Church which appeared certain to creak and crack as gaudily as the baroque courts and painted kings of a gasping past. But while pietism was a religion which made nonsense of anything other than the experience of grace, the pious construction of Kant was a religion of every experience but grace. He would refuse to make sense of nonsense. And in that

---

[3]Stanley Jaki, *Angels, Apes and Men* (La Salle, Ill.: 1983), pp. 33, 106 n. 39.

is something of the Jansenist's foe known as Quietism; for while the Jansenists and their Protestant counterparts identified grace with sensible emotion, the Quietists looked on sensible emotion as a moral defect. Though Kant refused to be called a Deist with good cause, his eclectic system provided the somewhat stern hospitality of a half-way house on the road from the Deism of Locke to the Liberalism of the nineteenth century. And so it came to pass that the tone of what was considered the right intellectual life in a post-Kantian world would have all the notes of a moral religion except God.

No malice in Kant squeezed traditional doctrine of its plausibility. The decline of doctrinal articulation was more the product of an exaggerated devotion to private judgment as the arbiter of essential Christianity. Nothing could be more anachronistic than to think Kant posed as a "post-Christian." The post-Christian rarely does. To his labyrinthine way of thinking, Christianity is the only cogent and moral religion, and other kinds of religion are servile attempts to bribe favors from fanciful supernatural powers. Readily, though, did he assume the mantle of a rehabilitator superior to a reformer; the spirit of Christianity would be revived in a manner conformable to the human autonomy which had finally asserted itself in the glare of clarity. If any critical chorus tried to paint his particular God as reason itself, he could protest that his humble aim and reverent exercise was to make the truths of Christianity reasonable. A religion, he said, which imprudently declared a wild war on reason would lose.

Taking him at his word, none can deny that his effort launched a demythologizing of grace which did not nurture religion within the limits of reason alone, but smothered it. A certain halting nobility, almost painful in its deliberation, attaches to Kant's critique of religion and its limits. It is impressive in its consistency if consistency is not humbug, sober in its obligation to name the consequences of its case, sturdy in its willingness to remain unconsoled if those results proffer few consolations, and sympathetic in its zeal for moral authenticity unweakened by convention. It only slips when, having bid religion accept its limits, it turns coy about the limits of reason. For reason alone is more than a lonely thing; it fast becomes an empty thing.

The Epistemological Argument

Religion Within the Limits of Reason Alone is less optimistic than earlier works, and this is all to the good if optimism admits to being hope bereft of its ultimate object. But Kant makes no such admission. He is only shifting diction to treat a more solemn case: the complexities of evil in a rational universe.   This persuades him to vindicate more stridently the autonomous self through the exercise of reason alone as reason undefiled. It is the mental ability to provide *a priori* knowledge, pure in its independence of experience.

Before Leibniz (1641-1716) who maintained that reason is capable of objective knowledge free of the human limits of perspective (the classical school of rationalism), and Hume (1711-1776) who questioned such confidence and held that all knowledge is subjective because it comes by experience, thus making objective understanding of the world impossible (the school of empiricism), Descartes (1596-1650) had posited the question of objective knowledge in stark anthropocentric terms, albeit it with a Christian profession.   In contrast, traditional realism does not accept the subjective-objective dichotomy. The natures of real things are expressions of God's creative intelligence, and the human intellect is capable of understanding those natures, at least to a limited degree. A crucial difference in epistemology lies in the recognition of a higher "Subject," God. But from the Cartesian background, aware of problems in the rationalism of Leibniz and Wolff, Kant found not much more satisfaction in Humean scepticism; yet its two central tenets became his as well. First was that the agency of reason alone does not suffice for knowledge; and secondly, intuition provides the basis for cognition but does not constitute knowledge *per se*. Knowledge of reality requires a personal intuition of it, and a rational interpretation of that intuition. The entire dance of modern introspection would come to circle around the attempted resolution of so delicate a puzzle.

Stepping to the front of the stage, Kant unveiled a plot for reason and experience, showing their respective roles and describing the degree of cognitive objectivity they must provide. But in matters of religion, the looming question of belief is a challenge to the workability of this scheme. As knowledge of God is *a priori* and also synthetic, reason as distinct from understanding can only posit God as a regulative ideal.

So certain a man as Kant was particularly certain of this: theology cannot be trusted to itself because of its commitments to propositions beyond the realm of unassisted reason. What then? He commends his work as a purely philosophical theory of religion, presenting its relation to human nature in terms of rational synthesis. His focus rests on what Biblical theologians would call the chief anthropological mystery: the presence of good and evil predispositions in the human fact.

The four essays of *Religion Within the Limits of Reason Alone* present these predispositions as nothing less than "two self-subsistent active causes influencing men." The diction, certainly in the Introduction, is didactic, volunteering philosophical services to theologians with a salute, but the sort of salute which begins a duel and not a conversation: "For the sciences derive pure benefit from separation, so far as each first constitutes a whole by itself; and not until they are so constituted should the attempt be made to survey them in combination." His own slant is evident from the outstart as he addresses Biblical theologians, who may be divided into pastors or "divines," and scholars, though some may be both. For he does not address the natural theologian, the very notion of which, though prominent in Catholic method, is to Kant a contradiction in terms.

Even before starting his four essays, he has made known however obliquely that theology cannot be referred to nature, but exclusively to morality. There can only be a moral God, and reason cannot prove a God beyond a system of moral associations. The *Critique of Pure Reason* had already attacked the scholastic arguments for the existence of God: ontological, cosmological, and even the argument from design which is lyricized as a tribute to an architect but not evidently of a creator. There comes a point when Kant says flat out: "God is the moral-practical reason legislating for itself."[4] The eschatological portent of good and evil is absent from the start, and the cosmic Christ a non-entity.

Then it is predictable that the first three considerations of good and evil in relation to human freedom will issue, as have modern attempts at de-supernaturalization, with an assault on the mystery of the Church as mediator of grace. Coming to the defense of Kant against metaphysical empiricists who invariably treat his philosophy of immanence as totally subjectivist, Albert Leclere of the University of Berne in 1902 painted this as a misunderstanding of what Kant meant by objective reality, that he did oppose Berkeleyan idealism and did mean by "object" other than what Aristotelian epistemology means. As Leclere would have it, the Kantian "object" is rather the relationship obtaining between the mind of the knower and the Aristotelian object.[5] But if this is so, it does not alter the stridency of Kant's own final account of the ecclesiastical system of supernatural agency in the duel or dance between faith and reason.

Hobbes fired the mental shot of a revolution when he rejected the classical concept of natural law in favor of a totally empirical nature. It was also a modern sort of revolution in its

---

[4]Immanuel Kant, *Opus Postumum* 1:145.

[5]Vid. Gabriel Daly, *Transcendence and Immanence* (Oxford: 1980), p. 46.

pessimistic primitivism. In his wake, modern determinism and statism made ever grayer and dimmer the Epicurean assumptions which Hobbes had appropriated. That this candidate for natural law has regularly been confused with the classical notion of a primary norm in the human conscience is, as Maritain regretted, one of the oddest and most unfortunate mistakes of intellectual historians.[6] Rousseau added to this empiricism an almost cultic enthusiasm for individualism and the moral life (hypocritically conjoined to an authoritarian statism) which then grafted itself onto the Kantian experiment.

The Rousseauan contempt for original sin as a blasphemy against nature had a certain cogency for Kant long before his *Religion*, and one should not underestimate the significance of Kant's decision to hang a picture of the eccentric French sage in his stark study. Maritain may be too blithe about the influence of the prophet of the Noble Savage upon the dramatist of Pure Reason; he calls its emotional rather than philosophical. The sentimentalism of Rousseau was awkward for the mechanical compulsive, but Kant nonetheless freely testified that the man "set me right." In the *Opus postumum* he even ventures a scheme worthy of Rousseau: henceforth all his efforts must be to intellectualize the content of worth beneath the sludge of primitive importunity so that he might complete the restoration of "the rights of man."

The apologetic of human autonomy, then, replaces anything like a traditional theodicy as a frame of reference in treating of grace. And so Kant has already begun what will become, much more than the systems of Hobbes and Hume, the most radical alteration in the course of moral philosophy since the Renaissance. All that a sociologist would call a moral revolution in the twentieth century, which must include all life issues from sexual ethics to bio-technology, has a lineage reaching back to that initial Kantian trauma which placed morality in the line of

---

[6]Jacques Maritain, *Moral Philosophy* (New York: 1964), p. 94.

duty rather than in the line of the good. The Kantian discourse confines itself to acquired moral virtue (that is, natural virtue acquired by efforts of the will), and has no category for infused moral virtue (that which is produced directly in the soul by God).[7] The categorical imperative is to "Do that through which you become worthy to be happy." Thus a purely philosophical ethic becomes the abstract instrument of what has come to be called secularization. Divinely revealed moral structures and capacities were replaced with a philosophical moral theory which functioned as the sole judge of what is authentic in the interior life of religion. The moral universe of Kantian perception consists wholly of the interior receptivity of the conscience cut off from the empirical perception of objects and the desire for beatitude manifest in beholding God as God.

What Kant means by happiness in the categorical imperative is not that beatitude which, in the traditional Christian economy, is the end of the life of supernatural grace, and which is motivated be a desire for the good. Happiness is made the object of desire "that can be satisfied by nature in its beneficence."[8] This does, however, require a harmony between sentient nature and the moral law, and such harmony does not obtain: "Nature has not taken (man) for her spiritual darling." Thus the stress on duty to moral principles becomes paramount, and its practice has to be the ground of happiness. So it cannot be said that he banishes happiness from the stately halls of morality. Schleiermacher in fact rejected Kant's association of happiness and virtue because happiness, he insisted, is a response to time and senses and these are not in the line of reason. (Schleiermacher would allow no decorations in the sober corridors of his moral world.) When Kant says, "Pure reason does not require that we should renounce the claims of

---

[7]Cf. Jaki, op. cit., pp. 28ff.

[8]Immanuel Kant, *Critique of Judgement*, trans. Bernard (New York: 1970), p. 353, hereafter *CJ*. On infused virtue, vid. Philip of the Holy Trinity, *Summa Theologiae Mysticae* (Paris: 1874), vol. 2, pp. 45-46.

happiness," he requires that happiness be in proportion to virtue.[9] Virtue is the worthiness to be happy, and the Stoic and the Epicurean alike are taken to task for making virtue and happiness seem the same, whether one calls virtue happiness or makes happiness the very definition of virtue.[10] It may well be that this is what Maritain means by the Stoic deification of moral virtue, by which virtue became a naturalistic savior safeguarding life from futility.[11]   And Schleiermacher may not have appreciated the subtlety of Kant's own distinction.   Yet the Kantian relationship between virtue and happiness is not authentically Christian, either. The orthodox vision is neither Stoic nor Epicurean, but this is so in tribute to a beatitude which is the end of moral life. Christian beatitude is neither virtuous happiness nor Kantian dutifulness. It is absolute happiness attained through love of the Good for the very sake of the Good. In Christianity this is a supernatural agency of grace, the animation of the human desire by the divine will. But as this is other than morality lived through the agency of reason alone, Kant considers it self-serving and egocentric. Thus his rejection of infused virtue.

The Kantian concern was for a noble detachment from rewards. Here, again, Kantianism shows its quirky affinity with Quietism. But as sharp critics of these things, like Balthazar, hasten to comment, once disinterestedness is presented as virtuous only as a function of pure reason, it radically parts company with Christian beatitude which locates it in love. Our contemporary equivalent should be obvious: the claim to a detached motive appeals to the secular humanitarian, but unless the motive is ordered to the pursuit of a sovereign Good it becomes self-defeating. Without God as their proper object, faith becomes credulity or incredulity; hope becomes optimism or pessimism; love becomes eroticism or cruelty or both. Does not

---

[9]*CJ*, p. 199.

[10]Cf. John R. Silber, Intro. to *RWLRA*, p. cxiii.

[11]Maritain, op. cit., p. 56.

the easy transition from the facile good will of the 1960's Hippie to the cynicism of the 1980's Yuppie offer a social montage of the degeneration? Real disinterestedness is attained according to the order of finality. Kantianism then provides a place for the virtuous person but not for the saint. And such a one soon enough becomes less like Quintilian's good man and more like St. Paul's clanging cymbal.

Kant was something of a retentive crank, and neighbors could time the day by his household habits and excursions; but he was not unsympathetic for that. He granted the need for self-interest in everyday matters, in attention to health and so forth, though one gets the impression that any feast will be on vitamins. The formal motive for an act remains exclusively the law, the imperative summons of duty. Here lies the contrast between natural virtue and sanctity, and it has eluded the modern post-liberal mentality as it did the Enlightenment. Beatitude remains the definitive prospect and purpose of the Christian moral life, and when it does not appeal to virtuous people, as it did not appeal to Kant, a cause may lie in how it is suspect as a form of solipsism or simplistic eudaemonism, and boring for that. As the Eton schoolmaster, Mr. Headlam, is said to have put it: "Doubtless I shall inherit eternal bliss but I prefer not to contemplate so melancholy a proposition."

The incipient melancholia, however, lurks in the Kantian imperative of duty as an end in itself; supernatural grace finds no play, and divinity itself becomes a pedantic proposition hardly capable of inspiring any length of happiness. Kant's God, after all, attracts a cold mental calculus, for nothing else could be inspired by a divinity constructed of the moral-practical reason legislating for itself. The demythologization of grace introduces a hyper-moralism whose chief tragedy is worse than making the moral life merely a duty; it makes the prospect of heaven tedious. Here are the underpinnings of the Social Gospel and Liberal Protestantism which were convenient to progressivist optimism until they were exposed by the harsh glare of modern realities.

The conceit can fairly be traced to the Kantian inability to provide a supernatural exegesis for Christ's admonition: "No one is good save my Father." (Matt 19:17) Kant never successfully reconciles it with the command, "Be perfect as my Father in heaven is perfect." (Matt 5:48) He has built his own trap: having located satisfaction in phenomenal (temporal) reality, how can he still acknowledge hope for happiness in the noumenal life?[12] Whatever the clarity of his purpose, Kant assembled a moral pattern which must end in an opposition of happiness to virtue; at least the headmaster who thought heaven melancholy would have had the sympathy of Dr. Kant.

Nature

Any consideration of ends eventually raises two questions, and they remain the seminal questions in contemporary debate about human beings and God: what is the condition of nature (in which some sort of happiness is to be found), and what is the character of human freedom (the proper end of which in the gift of grace is beatitude)? The Christian order of grace and supernatural agency works within an explicit creation which is both fallen and redeemed. It also exacts obedience as an act of free will to participate in the benefits of redemption, the ultimate benefit being eternal bliss. Kant, and his heirs in philosophy, parted company with revealed Christianity on both accounts.

Kant was too much a creature of the Enlightenment to accept the judgment of the Fall of Man against an unstained nature, yet integrity bound him to the judgment of historical experience against the optimistic moral tradition which stretched from Seneca to Rousseau. He proposes a compromise at the start of Book One: "The conflict ... is based on a disjunctive proposition: Man is (by nature) either morally good or morally

---

[12]Cf. Greene, Intro. to *RWLRA*, p. lxiv.

evil. It might easily occur to any one, however, to ask whether this disjunction is valid, and whether some might not assert that man is at once both, in some respects good, in other respects evil. Experience actually seems to substantiate the middle ground."[13] But he does not extend this to an ontological fact of nature. This is a subjective moral condition, for to locate good and evil in natural impulses is assumed to deny human freedom: "... We shall ever take the position that nature is not to bear the blame (if it is evil) or take the credit (if it is good) but that man himself is its author."[14] And in this sandy soil is rooted the ephemeral moral naïveté of modernism: "(Man's) being good in one way means that he has incorporated the moral law into his maxim; were he, therefore, at the same time evil in another way, while his maxim would be universal as based on the moral law of obedience to duty, which is essentially single and universal, it would at the same time be only particular; but this is a contradiction."[15] The reader will note how the hypothesis is made to fit the conclusion.

The Kantian jealousy for human autonomy in the created order was a defensive reaction, however roundabout, to the Lutheran portrait of a totally corrupt human nature. If Kant leaned to optimism where Catholicism moved in the line of hope, he was nonetheless more at home with the Catholic than the Protestant in measuring the damage of the human condition. But once faith and reason had been divorced in the Protestant critique, there was little chance that Kant could resume the scholastic attempt to synthesize the two. His solution was to separate the moral and natural universes even more; and this created an isolating psychological abyss which has been called perhaps the worst legacy of the Enlightenment.[16]

---

[13]*RWLRA*, p. 18.
[14]Ibid., p. 17.
[15]Ibid., p. 20.
[16]Cf. Colin Gunton, *Enlightenment and Alienation: Essays Toward a Trinitarian Theology* (London: 1985), p. 25.

Where Luther gave the prize to faith, Kant gave it to reason, ever deepening the divide between the material order and revelation. The modern inability to acknowledge the very concept of cosmos is an infection transmitted from the incubator of the Reformation. Kant's contribution was to invest reason with the whole function of interpreting the meaning of good and evil. Reason in fact became the essential litmus of the moral life, or as Colin Gunton puts it, a Procrustean bed for all judgment.[17]

Scholastic epistemology understood reason as a natural light from God which is strengthened in the natural order and raised to participate in God's knowledge through the grace of faith. Thus God reveals truths which are accessible to human reason, but which are necessary for salvation and could not be known by many men in the present order (since they lack the capacity or time, and they would likely fall into serious errors about these matters.) In a challenge to the very heart of the Scholastic spirit, Kant opposed faith to knowledge altogether, and reduced it to an indication of what cannot be known. In this sceptical alchemy lies a source of the modern suspicion that any supernatural account of grace and nature is illusory. Coleridge would try to repair this misadventure by making belief and understanding the same thing in different stages of growth. For Kant that would be ungainly sentimentality. Yet his own solution is hardly free of illusion as it combines empirical realism (the world of objects known to us is a real world and we cannot know of any world beyond it) and transcendental Idealism (the ideas by which we interpret nature are not the results of experience but occur *a priori*).

Kant was not a material, or empirical Idealist, if such means thinking that physical objects do not exist outside the mind. But for him space and time are only the forms of our intuition. Mental perception of space and time cannot be checked against extra-mental reality. Of course this has drastic consequences for

---

[17]Ibid., p. 6.

any kind of criticism touching upon the attentions of religion. Greek and Hebrew concepts of time are equally irrelevant, for instance, and the Bible is less an organic account than it is random and eclectic.[18] Any intimation of salvation history, or of history at all for that matter, broods as a deterministic threat to human freedom, and so it must be rejected. Once one allows this, there is no valid historical explanation for the fact of evil, certainly none for it as *privatio boni* in the Christian doctrine of atonement: there is "for us no conceivable ground from which the moral evil in us could have come."[19] Attempts to construct any such ground are rhetorical exercises: "We must not, however, look for an origin in time of a moral character for which we are to be held responsible; though to do so is inevitable if we wish to explain the contingent existence of this character (and perhaps it is for this reason that Scripture, in conformity with this weakness of ours, has thus pictured the temporal origin of evil)."[20] The inheritance of original sin and the continuing repercussions from the Fall of Man have nothing to do with reality: "IN the search for the rational origin of evil actions, every such action must be regarded as though the individual had fallen into it directly from a state of innocence."[21]

To ensure moral autonomy, the doctrine of original sin succumbs to a new doctrine of fundamental option, if one wants to put it that way, though the term was unknown to Kant. Whatever factors condition man's moral decision, "his action is yet free and determined by none of these causes; hence it can and must always be judged as an original use of his will."[22] As moral choices are original acts of each private will, evil is the desertion of maxims of duty for maxims of inclination. Or rather, it is less of an incentive distinct from good as it is the

---

[18]Ibid., pp. 114-115.
[19]*RWLRA*, p. 38.
[20]Ibid., p. 38.
[21]Ibid., p. 36; cf. p. 37n.
[22]Ibid., p. 36.

subordination of duty to irresponsibility. Circumstantially, judged by motive, the intelligible character can still be evil when the empirical character is good.[23] One wants to bear in mind, here, Kant's absolute commitment to the idea of the good, which saves his system from becoming the superficial kind of situationalism found in some contemporary moral theologies. The Kantian concept of evil forms along with goodness the two elementary features of human character even though, as indicated, they are not co-equal once a man has chosen the moral law for his maxim. Evil then becomes an incident which violates the dutiful maxim.

De-mythologization so radical as this is actually an intense re-mythologization. And this is inevitable within the context of an historical religion once history is denied as authentic.[24] A religion formed of myths can only be dismantled once the myths are denied; a religion formed of what it claims are facts can only be made a different kind of religion once the facts are denied. The very denial becomes mythic, as an exaltation of the power to deny. The Incarnation, for instance, becomes the realization of a moral ideal strengthened by its independence from the miraculous; tragedy does not replace comedy but claims to be the maturity of comedy; Jesus is not a divine archetype but the human archetype of duty, the "man for others" whose "otherness" consists in being a man "for others" rather than coming "to others." That archetypal condition is accessible to all humans through the guidance of pure reason in the natural order and not through pure obedience to a supernatural order.

If this borders on caricature, it disserves Kant who keenly recognizes that Christian faith "being historical, rightly starts with the belief in atonement."[25] But that same voice rejects all theories of temporal atonement and limits the consideration to moral symbol. To remove religious faith from the appeal of

---

[23]Ibid., p. 32.
[24]Greene, op. cit., pp. x-xi.
[25]*RWLRA*, p. 109.

historical experience and to confine it to the deepest recesses of moral consciousness, indeed to evade the historical perspective of human origins, was to be genuinely a creature of the Enlightenment; but it also was to be the creator of a half-Christianity in which divine acts are irrelevant to natural experience. This is not to impute bad faith to Kant, or to deny the dignity of his intentions; it is simply to contrast the Kantian denial of the certitude about historical revelation with the Catholic denial of any means other than revelation to comprehend properly the economy of grace.[26] Having said that, one should not think that only a minor difference is at stake between Kant's denial of natural theology and the Church's affirmation of it. Kant's position on human reason completely precludes the very possibility of revelation in any realistic form. The menace is not so much a contradiction of supernatural faith, as it is a denial of the natural knowledge which prepares the way for the grace of faith. Kant will not allow grace to build on nature and to perfect man's created capacity to know.

Kant summarily and severely denies to revelation truths inaccessible to human reason. From his pragmatic point of view, revelation at best only makes easier the perception of what can be discovered naturally. It is true that "without a belief in God reason would have to regard the moral laws as empty figments of the brain."[27] But non-rational metaphysics can only redefine the proper spheres of the sciences. The moral life is the preserve of reason in the Kantian picture of things, stained glass unstained so that clear light may confound the darkness of the intellect.

The moral law which duty obliges has the authority of divine revelation for Kant, inasmuch as it is perceived through pure reason, issuing in an ethical commonwealth parallel to a political one, a Kingdom of God which is ethico-civil as the political

---

[26]Cf. eg. Con. Vatican I. *Dei Filius*, II; Pius X, Encycl. *Pascendi*; Pius XII, Encycl. *Humani generis*.

[27]*CPR*, p. 811.

commonwealth is juridico-civil.[28] Established in splendid isolation by the *fiat* of moral law, and not decreed by supernatural agency, this shining order is a glimmer of the Kingdom of God animated by the presence of Christ. But the glimmer can be hypnotic, and hypnosis is not revelation. Maritain warned how dangerous it is to be half-Christian.[29] If, as Kant supposed, the religious idea "rises out of morality and is not its basis,"[30] then the moral life attains to a sacralization, and its jealousy for autonomy pretends to quixotic omnipotence.

It will then happen that moral motivations claim a divinity of their own architected by the craft of reason. And in the construction of that heady edifice, reason sacrifices one thing, but that thing is wisdom. Long before that loss, however, Kant had denied what is evident: that men naturally reason from things they know through their sense to the existence of their First Cause. As with so many of the rationalists, the final conclusions are splendidly consistent with their initial assumptions; but the initial assumptions have not knocked on the door of reality. Chesterton fittingly said in his *Varied Types* that such logicians "tend to forget that there are two parts of a logical process, the first the choosing of an assumption, and the second arguing upon it, and humanity, if it devotes itself too persistently to the study of sound reasoning, has a certain tendency to lose the faculty of sound assumption."

Kant unconsciously has sources in Scotus and Ockham and Descartes, and their attentions to the claims of free will. But as Maritain contends after marshalling an array of evidence, Kant's product devastated the development of culture; this was a supreme irony, given his exalted estimation of culture which was so unlike Rousseau's eccentric buffoonery on the subject. The damage was profound and it came because the denial that the moral law can be inferred from the revealed will of God caused

---

[28]*RWLRA*, pp. 87ff.
[29]Maritain, op. cit., p. 90.
[30]*RWLRA*, p. 5.

the opposite of what it wanted. It was not merely that Kant rejected the doctrine on Original Sin; the rejection was the result of much more radical neglect, namely the rejection of natural theology, disguised under the seemingly plausible theory that the knowledge of God is limited to *a priori* synthetic knowledge. Kant would secure the independence of the human spirit, but the outcome resulted in a despotic autonomy, the willful Will of Man under the guise of pure practical Reason.[31]

The despotism is in the concept of necessity. For Hume the mind responds to sense impressions and constructs a pattern of concepts necessitated by custom or habit. Kant's pattern also has to be the way it is. Having removed good and evil from historical categories, Kant made human will autonomous to the extent that it was free to devour itself. That is to say, by denying the dependency of the mind on the active agency of the material world, by denying any heteronomous moral authority, Kant in effect increased the moral isolation which he sought to resolve through an assertion of independent human reason. The consequent unreality perdured to the technological age, and a nonsense of alienation from the self has practically become the definition of Modernism.

Freedom

To the Kantian mind, the Christian doctrine of an external relationship between morality and the will of God (externalism) is a mistaken anthropomorphism, a mythified anthropology. The Kantian tries, in a manner which became the mode of late modern times, to denounce the "institutional Church," or what he called the *cultus externus*, as an infringement of essentially moral and interior Christianity. The ideal ethical community, which would absorb ecclesiastical convention and purify it, was

---

[31]Cf. Maritain, op. cit., p.91.

clothed with the romantic primitivism with which Rousseau
loosely draped all nature.   There would be no place for the
sacraments which provide the supernatural agency for grace.
Even Kant's commendation of public prayer is of a naturalistic
moral desire to cement communal structures, rather than dispose
the soul in the traditional pattern of prevenient grace.[32]

Kant's idea of worship resonates with the modern liturgical
emphasis of "building community" at the expense of cultic
sacrifice, the setting up of a static didacticism in the place of the
studied ritual acts of the Mass, and the unweighed importunity of
a vernacular diction.   These things and the confusion of
sacerdotalism   with   misanthropic   clericalism,   are   vividly
anticipated in Book Four, "Concerning Service and Pseudo-
Service Under the Sovereignty of the Good Principle, Or,
Concerning Religion and Clericalism." Kant finds the Christian
formula of prayer "nothing but the resolution to good life-
conduct which, taken with the consciousness of our faith, carries
with it the persistent desire to be a worthy member in the
kingdom of God."[33]

As for public prayer, his account is an argument for
translating intercession into wishful poesie; it "possesses in itself
a more rational basis than does private prayer for clothing the
moral wish, which constitutes the spirit of prayer, in a formal
mode of address — and it does this without picturing the
Supreme Being as present, or thinking of the special power of
this rhetorical device as a means of grace."[34] His remarkable
gloss, one clear example of the Procrustean-bed technique,
removes from the Our Father the essential petition and doxology,
its eschatological burden, and most significantly for his bias, the
request for forgiveness. He is more candid than most cynical
liturgical hobbyists of the present age: "Praying, thought of as an
inner formal service of God and hence as a means of grace, is a

---

[32]*RWLRA*, p. 185n.
[33]Ibid., p. 183n.
[34]Ibid., p. 185n.

superstitious illusion (a fetish-making); for it is no more than a stated wish directed to a Being who needs no such information regarding the inner disposition of the wisher; therefore nothing is accomplished by it, and it discharges none of the duties to which, as commands of God, we are obligated . . ."[35]

And what to be exact is the grace of which he speaks above? The word appears in about ten places in the book but the idea is consistent, once again revealing Quietist sources. Grace is a superior's decree conferring a good upon a subordinate who is nothing but morally receptive. It appears, and tellingly so, that he addresses actual grace; sanctifying grace, or the indwelling of the Holy Spirit, is not within the categories of this system, having been replaced by pure reason. In Kant's eyes anything else would compromise our autonomy and, thus, our moral agency; and it has been to safeguard that conception of moral agency that he has postulated, in Platonic fashion, a supra-temporal freedom founded on the theory of virtue as knowledge, of sin as ignorance, and a conviction that the knowledge of the good ensures performance of the good. If there are any hints here of the exaggerated "fundamental option" theory popular in heterodox moral theology today, they are only further evidence of that disposition by which assertions of autonomy abolish true moral freedom.[36] For the plain assertion of autonomy fails to dispose the soul to receive the grace in the temporal order to conform to external divine will. Though it is supposed to, the autonomy of which Kant speaks obviously does not confer a certitude which the Church claims, and which perforce seems inscrutable and arrogant to the Kantian: ". . . we remain wholly in the dark as to when, what, or how much grace will accomplish in us . . ."[37] The same voice seeks relief in some assurance that any other claim is fanatical.[38] Thus his eccentric appropriation of

---

[35]Ibid., pp. 182-183.
[36]Cf. Maritain, op. cit., p. 40.
[37]*RWLRA*, p. 179.
[38]Vid., Ibid., p. 162.

John 3:8 to justify demythologization: "The wind blows where it will, and thou hearest its sound but dost not know where it comes from or where it goes. So is everyone who is born of the Spirit."

Kant accuses the doctrine of transcendent grace, or of an heteronomous authority imposed on free will, of doing four classes of damage: claims to works of grace cause fanaticism, alleged experiences of grace cause superstition, supposed enlightenment causes specious illumination, and the various means of grace cause thaumaturgical aberrations of reason.[39] What had been supposedly a measured discourse on the excellence of reason becomes impassioned on the subject of objective grace; and this is so not only in the final accusation against corrupt ecclesiasticism, but it is unmistakable in his specific treatment of the central doctrines surrounding atonement and absolution. Absolute freedom precludes the possibility of grace, the granting of which in any event would compromise the moral motivation. Vicarious atonement, he holds, plainly offends moral justice: "But that a heavenly *grace* should work in man and should accord this assistance to one and not to another, and this not according to the merit of works but by an unconditional decree; and that one portion of our race should be destined for salvation, the other for eternal reprobation — this again yields no concept of divine justice but must be referred to a wisdom whose rule is for us an absolute mystery."[40]

Unwilling to abandon altogether so important a doctrine as atonement, he redefines it as a derivative of the moral archetype lying in the practical reason. With faith it becomes a sign of how one can become pleasing to God through a good course of life. This, he is confident, avoids both superstition and naturalistic unbelief. But not being historical, it cannot effect forgiveness. For Kant this is no objection. It is as it should be, as he has

---

[39]Ibid., p. 48.
[40]Ibid., p. 134; cf. pp. 106ff.

posited an incompatibility between forgiveness and absolute freedom. Man might achieve grace by making himself worthy of absolution.[41] But as modern cultural neurosis obliquely testifies, the doctrine of absolute responsibility destroys the individual through the burden of guilt without the intervention of redemptive forgiveness. This is what Maritain means when he asserts that Kant's supra-temporal freedom becomes the prison of modern man; or, as the Second Vatican Council taught, it is what keeps man a question to himself.[42]

Kant does not surmount the obvious obstacle to all such protracted discourse: man is a creature and as such he cannot be an autonomous moral agent. Docility to the laws of nature's Creator is not servility as Kant would have it. As creature, man is consistent with his own nature by obeying these laws. This loftier obedience will seem servile only to a human will which chooses evil. Contrary to Kant, in the Christian order this obedience cultivates relative autonomy as it becomes interiorized as habitual grace. A properly functioning reason discerns the justice of the laws; it is aided by the love which pursues them.

The virtue of love is conspicuously absent from the Kantian critique. In his definitive treatise on religion and reason it is mentioned on only two pages of main text and in three footnotes. It appears only once as love of God, and that to dismiss it from the scope of moral reality.[43] A rationalist cannot trust the concept of unselfish love for another being; and he certainly has no confidence in what purports to be unselfish love for God. This would appear to be the case even with Kant's modifications of the rationalist spirit. It surely is the witness of the Gospel that love secures a greater freedom for moral acts than a categorical imperative ordered exclusively by rational agents' self-legislation.

---

[41]Ibid., pp. 62, 64.

[42]Cf. Silber, op. cit., p. cxxxii; Maritain, op. cit., p. 40; Con. Vatican II, *Pastoral Constitution on the Church in the Modern World*, "Gaudium et Spes," n. 21.

[43]*RWLRA*, p. 170.

Christianity decidedly does not abandon reason for love, for such would be carnal romance. There can be nothing more reasonable than love of the subsistent Good as the final end for which all moral choices of the good are intended. But having rejected finality, Kant has also rejected this reasonable morality.

He does not deny the historicity of the Scriptures, and he does not even deny the possibility of miracles, among which the diabolic confrontations he considers the most doubtful; but they are irrelevant to the function of true religion as a moral construction. The advice to clergymen on their use is patronizing to say the least. Dismissed then is the realistic ontologism of St. Paul's proclamation concerning the sons of God no longer "under the law." Historically, this does not denote superiority to the law; it means freedom from any burden of constraint. Christ's obedience to the cross was freely undertaken as the token of subordination to the Father (John 5:19) and this freedom of obedience, the paradoxical consortium of Christ's passivity and activity which is the heart of the Passion, has summary expression in the kenotic hymn of Philippians 2.[44] Kant's exegesis of it speaks only in terms of a personification of the Good Principle. He does not describe the Incarnation in such a way that it provides access to grace through obedience. That grace is substantially the supernatural agency by which humans become *consortes divinae naturae* (2 Pet. 14) goes unmentioned in his discourse; yet it is the traditional key to the autonomy in which Kant vests interest. Through submission to the demands of grace, man who is made "a little lower than the angels" becomes superior to them.[45] When Kant is done, all that is left of the kenotic mystery is the valiant, but fragile, assertion of the humiliation of Jesus as an incentive for man to raise himself to the ideal of "holiness." But such holiness is understood as right behavior and not divine communion.

---

[44]Cf. *RWLRA*, p. 55.

[45]Ps. 8:6; cf. *S. Th.* I a. 2ae, q. 113, a. 9.

Naturalization of the holy proceeds clearly and directly from the decision to exclude beatitude from the moral order of ends. By eliminating beatitude which is the subjective ultimate end of being, Kant formally eliminates the love of that God who is the absolute ultimate. And for this, Maritain labels Kantianism the definitive hedonism, as it denies happiness the possibility of transcending itself. The moral agent receives no grace and expects no grace. As Maritain says in a plain description of the secularized moralist: "It is rather he who gives, who presents to the supreme Being acts whose goodness is entirely independent of that Being. He makes a present of his rectitude and the purity of his intentions, to be recorded in the books kept by a God who is a kind of eternal Accountant or Notary charged with establishing the final balance between the absolute Disinterestedness of the moral act and the invincibly interested Appetites of nature."[46]

Summary

By retaining an idiomatic reference to grace, Kant seemed to allow a contradiction of his doctrine of interior moral autonomy over against an outer deterministic world. Yet for all practical purposes, "reason alone" is made to function in place of supernatural agency, notwithstanding the radical distrust of reason that is reflected in Kant's denying to theology the ability to reach beyond empirical knowledge. The new distinction between two worlds of phenomena and noumena only superficially matches the Christian discernment of natural and supernatural realms. As Henri de Lubac has reminded philosophers of religion repeatedly, within a sacramental universe that which is supernatural is best understood in existential terms as the manifestation of grace in history, and the

---

[46]Maritain, op. cit., p. 101.

idea of a "supernature" as a positive entity is a problematic post-mediaeval accretion to the doctrine of the supernatural, first spoken of as a category by Baius. Eric Mascall, while speaking freely of supernature, says with characteristic felicity: "... the doctrine of nature and supernature in Catholic theology does not mean that the two operate in isolation from each other, like two families living in flats on two different storeys of the same building separated by a sound-proof floor. On the contrary, supernature means the supernaturalization of nature, the elevation of nature by grace to a condition that it could not obtain by its own powers. Grace requires nature as the raw material in which it works, and its sole *raison d'être* is to do this. Thus St. Thomas Aquinas not only tells us that grace perfects nature without destroying it, but also that grace requires nature as its presupposition."[47]

An intuition of this may have moved Kant to his denial of practical application to the noumenal; but his resolution of how the noumenal then associates with things phenomenal was forced, by the de-mythologization of supernatural agency, to realign completely the distinction of realms. Holiness itself becomes a rather ephemeral ethicism, a soberly pious *pastiche* of the state of grace. Without the interaction of the transcendent and immanent in an objective sacramental economy, the transcendent ends up usurped by immanence. And this is quite justly called secularization, even though Kant had every intention of escaping both the rock of "naturalistic belief" and the hard place of "superstition." But as Kant's God is transcendent to the point of inaccessibility, the antinomy of realms could only be resolved in derivative Kantian thought, if not by a return to fideism, then by pantheism or the utter transmutation of God into the immanent force of history. In either naturalistic case, supernatural agency evaporates. This had already happened,

---

[47]Eric Mascall, *Via Media* (London: 1956), pp. 138-139; cf. *S. Th.* I i, 8 ad 2.

though, once Kant himself had denuded his remnant pietism of what sacramental allusions it had inherited from scholasticism. The result was a stark "moral Governor" and "Supreme Legislator" who was hardly the God of the Law and quite definitely a deification of the Law.

Having proposed to popular thought and practice the identity of religion and morality, it was only a matter of time before Kantianism would give way to Hegel's ontological confusion of God and man, and his ominously banal translation of the drama of good and evil. Wholly opposite was the vision of the Second Vatican Council which spoke of "the world which is the theater of man's history, and the heir of his energies, his tragedies and triumphs; that world which the Christian sees as created and sustained by its Maker's love, fallen indeed into the bondage of sin, yet emancipated now by Christ, Who was crucified and rose again to break the strangle hold of personified evil, so that the world might be fashioned anew according to God's design and reach its fulfillment."[48]

Kantian autonomy, defined as it is by transcendental scepticism and epistemological relativism, rejects the core doctrine of grace according to which human freedom is the creation, and not the victim, of divine causality. For Kant, divine causality broods as a threatening contradiction of autonomy because of its externality.   This parts with the Christian description of divine causality acting gratuitously and not of necessity within human freedom: "It is God who, in his good will toward you, begets in you any measure of desire or achievement." (Phil. 2:13)

By this authentic cohesion of freedom and causality, evil, which is a lack of good, is also a privation of being, and as privation it has no divine cause. Now this is a more volatile and adventurous analysis than the Kantian account of good and evil as coexistent defects; and it presents the possibility of a

---

[48]"Gaudium et Spes," n. 2.

sanctification, or "fulfillment," far more compelling from the long historical perspective than Kant's identification of moral self-assertion with freedom from oppression. According to Kant, the pure reason, by resolving the inclination of the evil defect, practically takes the place of God. In the Pauline comparison with Adam, Christ "did not count equality with God a thing to be grasped." (Phil. 2:6) But Kant's project was of a sort more sophisticated than the temptation of Adam, though part of the continuum of pride, for Kant moves beyond the promise of equality to invite identity. And in this lies a voice whose timbre thrilled the modern conscience and then became its dismay. Instead of saying "I will not serve," Kantianism says "I will serve" and then it serves the self.

Kierkegaard on Existentialism

A Psychology of Truth

Theologians have made a truism of the distaste in the twentieth century for linear thinking, or verbal formulations of truth according to a logical process. In large measure, propositional theories repose wherever the nineteenth century reposes; but like the century, they have gone. The reaction of radical existentialism has been to deny an existence to objective truth altogether. A more sober tendency has been to judge theological truth as objective but not as a remote object of speculation; it is real according to the way it serves the personal reality of Christ. Søren Kierkegaard (1813-1855) asks, "What is truth, and in what sense was Christ the truth?" And his own answer comes: "Christ is the truth in such a sense that to be the truth is the only explanation of what truth is."[1]

Thus philosophy and theology are more intertwined the more personalism and objectivity participate in each other's definition. Copenhagen was not the first venue of the question: philosophers and theologians had their definitive encounter in Jerusalem, where Jesus Christ led Pilate to a certain level of discovery in a tradition which was as Socratic as it was rabbinic. But from that point, the answer is found in the man Christ, and not in any theory detached from the fact of the man. As Kierkegaard would say in ways complex and various, "The truth

---

[1] Søren Kierkegaard, *Training in Christianity*, trans. W. Lowrie (Princeton: 1944), p. 199.

consists in nothing else than the self-activity of personal appropriation."[2]

In the propositional pedantry of a defensive frame of mind, Pontius Pilate will not appropriate Christ this way; his wife has come close to doing so through a dream, but Pilate does not oblige. He confines himself to objective reflection, and asks "What is truth?" At once his helplessness is advertised to history: the question is asked of thin air, and there is no answer to an apostrophe. So far as Kierkegaard is concerned, the subject has become accidental, as it must when we try to be objective apart from involvement. Objective truth would be possible only if "being" were complete and the thinker could judge the conformity of thought and being from the vantage point of one outside himself. But Pilate's throne is not lifted up high enough to view *sub specie aeternitatis*. He knows full well, and lucklessly so, that he is *sub lege*. And as under the law, he detaches himself from the truth presented to human judgment in human form. The handwashing scene represents everything Kierkegaard detested in petty clericalism and bourgeois philosophy. The agony of Pontius Pilate is his incapacity for agony. He is a forebear of the erastian Bishop Mynster, known to Kierkegaard, who like many a modern cleric resolves dilemmas of the mind before God by reducing God to a plastic symbol, and calling the fantasy realism.

Where previous rebels based their anti-clericalism on the evidences of corruption and social hypocrisy, Kierkegaard based his on a philosophical complaint against the spiritual sloth of theologians who rejected the Cross of Christianity for the Comfortable Pillow of Cynicism. Pilate also resembles the romantic Hegel. For by not entering passionately into the truth, he condemns the Incarnate Truth himself to a passion whose unspeakable benefits he cannot reap.

---

[2]Søren Kierkegaard, *Concluding Unscientific Postscript*, trans. D. F. Swenson (Oxford: 1945), p. 182, hereafter *Postscript*.

Man must not approach truth as though it were a convenience, because man is not convenient to truth. He is a complex of history and his own ambiguous psychology. Descartes had exalted mathematics as the model of knowledge in its lucidity and reliability, unfettered by the circumstance of time or the bias of perception. But Kierkegaard swiftly and completely rejected the application of a mathematical hermeneutic to the human condition. People do not work that way. This psychology was not contrary to the Thomistic definition of truth: "adaequatio intellectus et rei." The agreement, or correspondence of thought and reality, can also be translated "adequacy." Thought, or expression, is true when it is adequate to the subject, when it makes itself clear to the experience of the knower.[3] Kierkegaard's objection to rationalism contested the Cartesian angelism which did not understand properly the psychology of the subject. Thus, as did come to pass in the nineteenth and early twentieth centuries, the quest for the "Essence of Christianity" would lead either to fundamentalistic literalism, or to the tedious moralizing of Liberalism. Both underestimated and ill-served the tremendous mystery of the human person. When Kierkegaard approached the deep subjects of existence, he virtually succumbed to a wild chiaroscuro of nights and days, offering his limited circle a depiction of the moral universe which could hardly have seemed more bizarre to the complacent Danish State Church.

Among his literature, the basic themes of a short life stand out in three pseudonymous works, offering the vision of faith greater than a function of texts or a diagrammatic moral system. These come to us as *Either-Or*, *Fear and Trembling*, and *Repetition*. In 1844, the dialogue of Socrates and Christ in the *Philosophical Fragments* addresses the historical context of salvation; and *The Concept of Dread* develops the consequences of this fear, or

---

[3]Cf. John Macquarrie, *Thinking about God* (New York: 1975), pp. 23-24, 39.

presupposition of sin, in time. Interspersed with his series of *Edifying Discourses* and psychological and literary portraits are *Stages in the Way of Life*; the difficult existential response to Christ in *The Concluding Unscientific Postscript* which is a full development of the *Fragments* on the objective and subjective problems of Christian truth; *The Sickness unto Death*, an etiology of despair; and the apologetical *Training in Christianity*.

Heightened diction and an anxious variety of conceits find a locus in two constant plots. And we deliberately say plots, for that suits the dramatic mode of Kierkegaard's exposition better than so propositional a fixture as a tenet. He is not content to make points or define tenets. His method is to use the elenctic dialogue of Socrates, setting aside critical assumptions individually, without directly constructing a thesis. When he makes points they are only devices in the crucial thematic involvement of the subject in truth itself.

The first theme, or plot, is the behavior of subjectivity (spiritual awareness). Specifically, this is the apprehension of divine truth through passion. Kierkegaard's terms have to be taken as he defines them, however eccentrically at times. And here there is also the disadvantage of working through the translation of a vocabulary which was difficult in the original; the Danish of the manuscripts concealed Kierkegaard from most of Europe until the lived dreadfulness of the First World War made him bewitching to those nations which had been made wastelands. Subjectivity, for example, does not carry its normal connotation.   Truth is subjective, but not as the denial of objective reality.   Objectivity is the very stuff of the soul's impassioned response. Kierkegaard means that objectivity is meaningless when isolated from personal experience. Truth must edify, but it does so radially through a rupture of lesser commitments.

The high truths of religion come, then, at a high cost in order to signify worth for a tragic existence. The mind can only know God's truth by making a total commitment to its consequences. Thinking is acting upon a risk. As an idea, this seems commonplace and even conventionally pious, but only because Kierkegaard has been so widely appropriated one way or another in late religious assumptions, as a kind of *demi-mondaine* update of the Catholic mystical tradition. But it is not an inescapable idea. Its absence from the clockwork regimen of Kant, and the imperviousness of Liberal smugness to its groan, shows it is not an obligatory principle of active minds. We may also betray a perspective, albeit a defensible one, by detecting it in the figure of Newman as he theologizes as by habit in response to an occasion, and involves his listeners in his idiom. And this is so even though his manner was as empirical and reserved as Kierkegaard's was *déséquilibré*.

The theme of subjectivity is developed in *Fear and Trembling*, written for Regine Olson. She was the young woman whose hand the elegantly bohemian writer finally denied himself; marriage was incompatible with his pathetic sense of an author's sacrifice. He embarked upon a chronic pattern of making his mortifications mortify others. The book is written as an allegory, an indirect communication, a literary evidence of the principle of hidden spiritual inwardness. Indirect communication serves the most profound truths which do not lend themselves to communication schematically. It is based on that stately maieuticism of Socrates, like a midwife coaxing thoughts already possessed obscurely. By indirect communication a tentative theory is being tested, and the reader has to think it out for himself. In his role of teacher in this process, the author's identity is irrelevant; the strength of the argument is left to rest on the argument itself. The highest form of indirect communication is "double reflection": the realization on secondary reflection that the truth "interests" one's existence. This inward appropriation cannot be delivered to someone by oral tradition; that someone is to go through the same interior process of appropriation. The technical word for appropriation is "reduplication": to exist in what one understands. It is the method of subjectivity, the response to a decision. And as such it is a living refutation of those two kinds of objective thought in religion: dispassionate speculation which remains aloof from the unique demands made by the Incarnation of Christ upon the soul, and tepid conventional "churchiness," or religion for religion's sake.

The second theme, the engine of Kierkegaard's strongest philosophical polemic, is the danger of Hegelianism. Hegel himself was not the target so much as were his idolatrous disciples, with their optimistic acquiescence to the present natural order and their clinical calculation. The synthetic system for which these ardent bores stood was, in Kierkegaard's estimation, the antithesis of the Christian promise. Hegelianism would represent the supremacy of creative reason, and its central figure is the dispassionate genius, brilliant with the blood drawn out, a pale power of humanity greater than any human, more android than superman. In the conceit was a ruinous sentimentality; Kierkegaard despised it and believed in no genius but a Savior covered with blood and full of torment. Christianity is not to be understood but to be done. The Hegelian's timid description of sin cannot make the feeblest response when asked to drink the cup of which Christ drinks. The Idealism of Hegel must then be rejected for it is mute in the face of the world's most humanizing challenge.

Kierkegaard's was a different Idealism, quite the contradiction of Hegel's. Here was an Idealism based on a definite characterization of the Platonized Socrates who finds the ideal in the real, instead of realizing the ideal. His university thesis had been about "The Concept of Irony, with Special Reference to Socrates"; the positive guide of Socrates, and the negative model of Hegel, became the co-efficients in his own philosophical formation. What he learned from the ancient Greek, as he could not expect to get from Hegel, was the infinite value of the eternal soul. Kierkegaard's rejection of Hegelianism in order to enter the subjectivity of existence, is commonly regarded as the first step toward modern existentialism. But when he walked away from Hegel, some of the Hegelian system stuck to his own method, and the chief remnant was the false concept of Idealism as a logic of reason. Kierkegaard thus felt obliged to abandon the rational mental governor when he tossed Idealism out. So far as he was concerned, the choice must be "Either-Or" in his own dialectic, either reason *or* faith.

His solution, however, does not lie in an anti-intellectualist manifesto of arbitrary will. Hegel's mistake had been to diminish the subject and the individual, and to exalt an objectivized subject; this was a self-contradiction in the eyes of Kierkegaard. Indeed, it indicates Hegel's ultimate blasphemy, the notion that a dialectic might refine contradiction into a smooth synthesis. Kierkegaard had another dialectic to offer, a "qualitative" one, continuously eliciting abstract distinctions, each negating, yet dependent upon, the other. So, for example, the qualitative dialectic holds in tension the facts of eternity and time, holiness and love, grace and responsibility.

The reader may remember how Kant, confronting such antinomies, fell silent and abandoned them to the noumenal world beyond reason. Kierkegaard confounds all Idealists by seeing them realistically as kinetic and creative. Doubtless, the qualitative dialectic cannot produce an intellectual schema of all existence, for only God is capable of that; but it can introduce the mystery of paradox. A paradox reminds the intellect of the infinite chasm between man and God, an abyss which Hegel's pride defied by identifying the human spirit with the Divine. That was the primeval delusion of man. We exist by divine fiat, Kierkegaard shouts out to his complacent companions, and the chasm is crossed only by way of the Cross and revelation. Vainly does Hegel relativize these symbols. His synthesis cannot taste the dreadfulness of divine disclosure, and so it misses its ineffable glory.

The qualitative dialectic seeks no synthesis. It vibrates between opposites in a state of perpetual paradox, and the tension gives life to the desolation of life itself.   The Philosophical Fragments, by being pieces, are meant to tease the pomposity of those Hegelians who offer the world an unfragmented system as a tidy package for all experience.   The author means to frustrate them with a dialectic rooted in transcendent paradoxicality which cannot be assimilated to any thought.   As Hegel drowns existence in pure thought and thus posits an unreal objectivity as truth, Kierkegaard counters with his doctrine of subjectivity as truth, subject to itself and not to a philosophy.

The obsession with the Hegelian crimes against the soul reached tragic proportions in a matter which would have seemed ridiculous to anyone less morbidly sensitive than this impassioned young figure.   He had been satirized by the Copenhagen comic journal, "Den Corsaren."   His defensiveness knew no bounds. Instead of ending his writing career, as he might have done once the Postscript had been handed in, he embarked upon deeper and more deliberately Christian musings without mincing words. Hegelianism is a pantheistic mimicry of Christianity. Moreover, Hegel had ignored the obligation of thought to a thinker; his system has only an idea of existence, and does not confront it as a fact.   Hegel smothers the struggle for truth in a quagmire of abstractions, and the substitute for the quest is an old Gnostic heresy puffed up and rouged for progressivist tastes.   As he viewed the Hegelians, Kierkegaard had the advantage of having learned their vocabulary, at the university during ten years of what had seemed to many at the time to have been a student's slumber.   He had been silent, but he had been awake.   And his eyes beheld an awful miscalculation in the Hegelian pretensions: in Christ indeed is the meeting of the finite and infinite, but Hegel saw in this a speculative identity of divinity and humanity when in fact it is a paradoxical unity of absolute qualitative differences.   Kierkegaard would enlist Hegelian distinctions (eg.

finite and infinite, temporal and eternal, nature and spirit) to refute any theoretical reconciliation of them.[4]

To the extent that this was a reaction to the supercilious confidences of the eighteenth century Illuminati, Kierkegaard was as much a romantic as Hegel, or Schleiermacher for that matter. There is no confession in him to that effect, and he mocks those who "see God in nature." A hike around the lakes with Coleridge and Wordsworth would have been a torture:

> ... Yes, Echo, thou great master of irony, thou who canst parody the highest and the deepest things on earth.... Yes, Echo, take vengeance upon all the nonsense which conceals itself in forest, in meadow, in church and theatre, and which now and again breaks loose and drowns out everything for me. I do not hear the trees in the woods relating to me old legends.... no, they whisper to me all the twaddle they have so long been witnesses of. I beg you in God's name to hew them down, so as to free us from those prating nature-worshippers. Would that all these prater's heads sat upon one neck; like Caligula, I should know what I had to do about it.[5]

An animal-rights activist could not have enlisted him in a crusade to preserve baby whales while ignoring human babies. But if romantics are subjectivists, Kierkegaard's different brand of subjectivity creates a whole new romance. The Hegelian absolute is not substance but subject. Schleiermacher is not so daring; he speaks of religion in more traditional terms, comparatively speaking, but the result is barely an intuition of the infinite, the feeling of absolute dependence. Kierkegaard would correct the undue stress of both. Hegel permits his absolute subject to obliterate the individual, so that it is indistinguishable from the absolute object; subjectivity yields to boundless

---

[4] Cf. Aage Henriksen, "Methods and Results of Kierkegaard Studies in Scandinavia" (Copenhagen: 1951), p. 145, in Paul Sponheim, *Kierkegaard on Christ and Christian Conscience* (London: 1968), p. 83.

[5] Diary, 2 Dec., 1837, in Walter Lowrie, *Kierkegaard* (Oxford: 1938), p. 100.

objectivity. But Schleiermacher is hardly less sanguine; his subjectivity had no toleration for paradox as the objective part of Christianity. If Kierkegaard is to be subjective, it will not be according to Schleiermacher's aesthetical feeling. The truest subjectivity, the most potent, is the passion of combined activity and passivity.[6] Out of this conviction then arises the crucial, and probably most misunderstood, declaration in the "Postscript" to the *Philosophical Fragments*: "The passion of the infinite is . . . subjectivity, and thus subjectivity becomes truth."

Levels of Existence

The passion by which subjectivity can claim to be truth is understood according to the three levels on which man can exist. There is nothing absolutely contingent or inevitable about them; they are much the evidences of deliberate decisions or, as Kierkegaard would say, decisions passionately made. Of necessity are they made passionately, because they are under the all-seeing eye of God making man ever more conscious of sin.

The first level is aesthetic. Here lies the carnal (though not necessarily sensual) man. "Eat, drink and be merry." He is uncommitted. His life lacks unity and meaning. He has no sense of duty or of married life. Predictably, his worst enemy is boredom. In refined form, this carnal figure was the typical disciple of Hegel. Kierkegaard's image for the Hegelian aesthete, or "Yuppie" of his day, is a stone skipping across the water, wave to wave, and then sinking the second it stops. The aesthetic life succumbs quickly enough to despair, and if he makes recourse to the finite he is doomed to a perpetual incompleteness, having refused to "put away childish things." But there is an alternative.

---

[6]Cf. James Brown, *Subject and Object in Modern Theology* (London: 1955), p. 36.

At the second level, cool detachment ends and the personality matures, involving itself in society and its institutions. This is a critical stage: personality realizes itself by "becoming" itself, or by making moral decision. And thus it opens itself to beauty and promise, things finer and more certain that the aesthetic *ennui* of the Hegelians. After his renunciation of marriage, Kierkegaard learned that man is condemned to remorse when this ethical experience is shattered. But shattering is inevitable for the maturing soul as it becomes conscious of a need for penitence. Fichte had no time for penitence; and this side of Fichte, interestingly enough, would later appeal to the Catholic Modernists, especially Tyrrell. To the moral Idealist, penitence must be wasteful and demeaning. Kierkegaard detects in it something else: the potential for both despair and belief in a brighter hope. Penitence, you could say, is a means of shattering not just oneself but the glass of intuitions through which one now sees darkly. The human passage from plain ethics to religion happens at this moment of decision, and it was precisely this moment that the future Liberals, Harnack and company, would shun with feigned bravado.

The third level of existence, the religious, is not hostile to the moral life; it provides an encounter with the Will behind creation which morality alone cannot afford. The highest of all passions is faith, and morality denuded of it is bewildered before paradox. Kierkegaard's favorite example, which is an oblique reference to his abandonment of Regine, is Abraham compelled to the morally wrong act of killing his son. In a "leap of despair," Abraham suspends the ethical norms to embrace the absurd. Now despair is melancholic doubt which seeks the consolation of faith to escape the unendurable. Faith itself is beyond the realm of reason, but by that fact, and not in spite of it, this faith represents the great paradox in the plausibility of absurdity: all things are possible with God. This is the reasonability of unreason. By faith in God's love, Abraham could yield to absurdity, clinging to the knowledge that Isaac would not be lost. And Isaac is restored to him.

Under the aegis of paradox, the man of faith rejects confidence in a logically or speculatively coherent view of existence. The man who loses his life will find it. Faith is a *coincidentia oppositorum*: paradoxical externally because no reasoning can attain to it, and paradoxical internally because the joy of it is born out of its pain. But the paradox of the absurd is not nonsense. As Newman will insist from the different vantage of his empiricism in the *Grammar of Assent*, nonsense is not mystery.[7] The mystery lies in the antinomy which obtains when finite intelligence approaches infinite reality.[8] Kierkegaard approves a line of Leibniz in commentary on this paradoxical demand of Christian experience contrasted to the mediating quality of philosophy: some things are above reason and some things are against reason. God cannot be known directly. The Word of God speaking words refracts into antinomies, and the authentic human response is impassioned involvement and astonishment.

Diastasis: The Wholly Other

Nothing animates and overwhelms this existentialism of faith as does the awareness of God's total apartness. The more we think we know him, the less we do.

> Every determination of his nature which makes God immediately knowable is indeed a milestone on the way of approximation, but one which marks an increase instead of a decrease in the distance; it does not measure toward the Paradox but away from it, back past Socrates and the

---

[7]John Henry Newman, *An Essay in Aid of a Grammar of Assent* (Westminster, Md.: 1973; orig. 1870), p. 46.

[8]H. R. Mackintosh, *Types of Modern Theology* (London: 1937), p. 234.

Socratic ignorance. This needs to be carefully noted, lest one experience in the world of the spirit what befell the traveller who asked if the road on which he was travelling went to London, because the Englishman had omitted to mention that he needed to turn about, since he was proceeding in the opposite direction.[9]

In the infinite qualitative difference between God and human nature, Hegel notwithstanding, thought and being cannot be one. Hegel posits nonsense because he will not imagine paradox. Reality is not learned by a doctrine of immanence; it is learned by existence. Indeed, it is constituted of existential paradox which thought cannot penetrate. Now this is the heart of what challenges the ontological argument of Anselm, and in turn the absolute Idealism of Hegel who supported Anselm in a way neither Aquinas nor Kant could:

The idea of demonstrating that this unknown something (God) exists, could scarcely suggest itself to reason. For if God does not exist it would of course be impossible to prove it, and if he does exist it would be folly to attempt it ... I always reason from existence, not toward existence, whether I move in the sphere of palpable sensible fact or in the realm of thought. I do not for example prove that a stone exists, but that something existing is a stone. . . ."[10]

To argue from existence is to become ever more aware of the diastatic disengagement of God and man. No single metaphysical system then applies to the theme, and certainly no natural theology can begin to unwind the mystery. "God is pure subjectivity, perfect, pure subjectivity. He has no objective being whatever in him; for everything that has such objective being comes thereby into the realm of relatives."[11] It is the venerable

---

[9]Søren Kierkegaard (pseud. Johannes Climacus), *Philosophical Fragments or a Fragment of Philosophy*, trans. D. F. Swenson (London: 1936), p. 52fn., hereafter *Fragments*.

[10]Ibid., p. 31.

[11]Søren Kierkegaard Papirer, XI 2 A54, in Sponheim, op. cit., p. 100.

doctrine of aseity: God is complete in his freedom from relative contingency. "God does not think, he creates; God does not exist, he is eternal. Man thinks and exists, and existence separates thought and being, holding them apart from each other in succession."[12]

Kierkegaard out-dramatizes the mystical apophaticism of such as Dionysius the Areopagite and Nicholas of Cusa. There is something as foreboding as forbidding in his dialectic. Faith would not be faithful if it could be demonstrated rationally, but it should nonetheless be available to the best of experience and empirical information. Or so the dissimilar voices of Aquinas and Kant agree. But Kierkegaard objects. In a profound irony of modern theology, his energetic denial of natural theology and the application of reason to revelation smoothed a path for the twentieth century's "Death of God" school. Many, if not most, of its teachers, were former Barthians who had inherited some of the diastatic critique. The "Wholly Other" of Kierkegaard's fevered dread is but one remove from the Non-God of more frigid thinkers. That "no man spake as he did" said something disturbingly compelling about Christ to him. But to Kierkegaard's remote heirs it could mean that Christ spake nothing.

That abuse of his legacy could not happen, Kierkegaard might have insisted, had these people respected the drama. Truly existential thinking removes the thinker from his tower and places him in the arena, in the *agone*, where he wrestles in a life or death struggle. In a later generation, the "Death of God" school would be inspired by a middle-class dislike of perspiration. But there were other theologians who were compelled by the titanism of the contest with far different issue: Jaspers and Heidegger most especially. Kierkegaard himself was content to make qualitative dialectic the ground of heroism in human life. By trying to harmonize it unrealistically, the Idealist becomes a

---

[12]*Postscript*, p. 296.

dilettante, a voyeur to human history. His refusal to engage the whole personality, and not the isolated intellect, in commitment, forfeits any claim to authentic existentialism. Kierkegaard's rejection of this fatuousness would later influence Barth's scorn for speculating clerks.

But the wild strokes of Kierkegaard's pen can lead to inconsistency. The spiritual regeneration moved by the existential decision does not truly restore the person to wholeness; it creates an utterly new personality. This is not a man being born again but another man being born; and yet all the while, the inwardness theory, or subjectivity, requires that man be himself in his docility to paradox and so attain to the wholeness of who he is. What clearer example of subjectivity could there be than the Magdalene's recognition of Christ when she hears her name on Easter morning? Kierkegaard's diastasis run riot is itself incapable of paradox here; for it denies the capacity of a boundless God to maintain contact with man even when sin had alienated man from him.[13] Man, after all, is in the image of God even though he is unlike God. And when Christ has harrowed Hell he returns and says, "Noli timere." To exaggerate the difference is to place a burden on apophaticism which the early Fathers of the Church would not. And it seems certainly so, that the "absolute Unknown" or "sheerly unqualified Being" is darker and more remote from the veiled *I Am* of the Temple.

We can see why Kierkegaard's description of the soul's dread in face of this Unknown can look like an abnormal psychology at work. And one does not have to be a doctrinaire Freudian to think his childhood seared itself into his account. The fantasy world which his father walked him through provided a lifelong security from outside evidences. It would border on superstition to call the circumstances of his death a pure coincidence; he collapsed holding the last of his unspent patrimony. In Copenhagen was a man who "went and hid his

---

[13]Cf. Mackintosh, op. cit., pp. 248ff.

master's money." We should not be surprised, then, when he
gnashes his teeth. The anguish, *Angest*, can be translated in a
pertinent modern psychologism as anxiety, *pace* Macquarrie after
Tillich, and was formed of a dread which became a philosophy:
"...dread is the dizziness of freedom, which occurs when
freedom gazes into its own possibility."[14] Kierkegaard's anxiety
was that of one matured in the third stage of development,
recognizing the great distance which sin had set between him and
his Creator.   His own awareness was heightened by the
complacency of the official Lutheranism which he had been
taught to his later disgust. He could have wanted a Bonhoeffer
or a Popieluszko in his pulpit, but all he got was an Establishment
liberal, Bishop Mynster in his suffocating contentment. It was
enough to test his mettle and even his sanity.

It is an understatement to say that Kierkegaard was not
given to understatement. Like the early Barth, he is almost
Manichean in his unaccommodating outline of idiosyncratic
demands in the Christian summons. But the hyperbole of despair
is not the raving of a madman, though it may be a most
calculating imitation of one, meant to stun the reader out of
static rationalism. The Kingdom of Heaven can be won, but the
course of the tournament requires a leap through fires of
tormented consciences. Rationalism inert in nature contradicts
the nature of becoming, which is kinetic literally as *kinesis*, a
dialectic of freedom and suffering. The *Philosophical Fragments*
assume the suffering character of coming into being. And since
the necessary cannot suffer, as suffering is the condition of
options, becoming is gratuitous, apart from any intrinsic
necessity, and is the activity of freedom:

> Nothing that comes into being does so by virtue of a logical
> ground, but only through the operation of a cause. The

---

[14]Søren Kierkegaard, *The Concept of Dread* (Princeton: 1946), p.
155, hereafter *Dread*. Cf. John Macquarrie, *An Existentialist Theology*
(New York: 1965), p. 68.

illusion provoked by the intervening causes is that the becoming is made to seem necessary; their truth is, that as they have themselves come into being, they ultimately refer back to a free cause. Even the possibility of deducing consequences from a law of nature does not indicate that any becoming is necessary . . .[15]

Fitting, then, is the motto he takes for his own: "Perissem, nisi perissem." The Cross stands as the interpretive escutcheon of the motto, and all sham variants of Christianity lodge in the refusal to carry it freely as the emblem of every authentic subjectivity. One could say that to "take up your cross" is the definitive existential appropriation of all life and all meaning. Again a paradox obtains: that this way of negation should be the way ordained by a loving God. Kierkegaard plunged into the paradox with full heart. But as he drifts more deeply into his quirky asceticism and the negativism of Schopenhauer, he seems nearly exhausted, close to surrendering the paradox of hope to the facile logic of pessimism.

The brooding becomes too self-conscious, as when he attacks Hans Christian Andersen for having said that genius needs comfort. What he might have thought of Lewis Carroll's domestic arrangements is not hard to imagine. Tyrrell called the "Alice" books his favorites, from an Idealism which turns upside down the subjectivity of Kierkegaard and its careful separation of absurdity from nonsense: ". . . there are times when our only chance of getting at truth is to throw off the heaped-up experience under which our child-mind lies buried, and to look at things with the fresh retina of our first consciousness ere fallacies of uniformity had crippled our freedom of perception."[16] The sentiment is redolent of the sentimental "story-telling" fad in contemporary exegesis; not that the concept is invalid in itself, but that it gives rise to a syndrome of comfortable reductionism, removing the objective historical demands of revelation, as

---

[15]*Fragments*, pp. 61-62.
[16]George Tyrrell, *Letters*, ed. Maude Petrie (London: 1920), p. 297.

though all salvation history in the end were an artificial cycle of satisfying impressions. That is why the Liberal, doubtful of religious certitude, would have struck Kierkegaard as one of the supreme *voyeurs* of the Incarnation. Liberalism would become to theology as intolerably bourgeois in its redefined contentments as Kierkegaard considered the portraiture of Thorwaldsen to be: the artist had left a picture of Christ, but the scandal of the Passion had been wiped from the subjective life of the Christian soul. There were no wounds, only hurt feelings. Confident that Liberalism was a halfway house on the way to atheism, Newman summed up its mutated Gospel with a Kierkegaardian diction:

> And you have caught some echoes of the love,
> As heralded amid the joyous choirs;
> Ye mark'd it spoke of peace, chastised desires,
> Good-will and mercy, — and ye heard no more;
> But, as for zeal and quick-eyed sanctity,
> And the dread depths of grace, ye pass'd them by.[17]

But is radical *Angst* in Kierkegaard a thing more dismal than the soul's unquiet according to Newman's orthodox mysticism? Maritain offers a warning, and it serves as a gloss as well on Newman's dictum that unbelief is as opposed to reason as is belief.[18] By an overwrought passion for the prospect of the annihilation of being, even philosophies which are not intrinsically hostile to religion may for all practical purposes be atheistic in method. "Perhaps this is why Kierkegaard, faced with an intelligence functioning in such manner, and, moreover, fully aware of the rights of reason, thought that faith exacted an anguished division of the soul and must always propose a perpetual challenge to reason."[19]

---

[17]John Henry Newman, *Verses on Various Occasions* (London: 1867), pp. 144-145. Cf. Newman, *Apologia Pro Vita Sua* (London: 1890; orig. 1864), p. 185.

[18]John Henry Newman, *Fifteen Sermons Preached Before the University of Oxford* (London: 1871; orig. 1843), p. 233.

[19]Jacques Maritain, *Range of Reason* (London: 1953), p. 206.

A belabored sense of anguish and pessimism about reason can become harsh and rigorist when it becomes a movement, and herein rests a subtle similarity between Kierkegaard's existential mood and the old Jansenistic determinism of grace, quite as there was something about Kant that could be at home with the passivity of the Quietism. As the Quietist measured spiritual vitality according to what consoled the senses, Kierkegaard cut a whole religion out of inconsolable longing; and when it was raised to an agony it pretended to the scale of virtue. The Dane began to lose sight of the proper end of holy desire as the classical mystics had not, and came to think that this myopia of grace was a new and unique insight, and that each of its blurs was a theophany. When one looks to the very different mental looms of Jansenists like Saint-Cyran and Arnauld two centuries before Kierkegaard, a similar flight from true ontology flutters the senses, thinking its subjectivism is real because it is so personal, and claiming to be honorable because it is intense.

More than a few of the same characteristics may be found today in attempts at spiritual renewal and updating when they are motivated by subjectivism. A peculiar self-consciousness can be carried to neurotic lengths in parochial and liturgical life once the life of reason becomes a burden to the "faith community." Some of its antecedent causes seem ever familiar, haunted by a — dare we say it — meretriciousness of faith: cynical toward spiritual gifts when they are truly gratuitous, and anxious for a reality which must be visible and audible to be certain. To cite but one instance, the Jansenist synod of Pistoia in 1786 objected to easily accessible and expeditious auricular confession, opposed statues of saints in church with their intimations of heavenly intercession, wanted that churches have only one altar and that this be plain, urged replacing Latin with vernacular texts, insisted on all of the priest's prayers being audible to the people, and removed infallibility from the Pope to the assents of the People of God.[20] Once a miscalculation of ontology reduces the drama of Redemption to the private theater of the ego, a common thread of morose egoism strings together Jansenism, Kierkegaard's Existentialism, and no less latter-day Modernism. The result for each is this: as the interior life passes through a spiritualist pathology, the redemption drama becomes a nervous theatrics, and the soul's ardor crumbles into a slowly smouldering hysteria.

A Conviction of Things Unseen

Unreconciled to the positive possibilities of endowed reason in the resolution of subjectivity, Kierkegaard provided Protestant neo-orthodoxy with some ammunition for the future: "With what industrious zeal, with what sacrifice of time, of diligence, of writing materials, the speculative philosophies in our time have laboured to get a strong and complete proof of the existence of God! But in the same degree that the excellence of the proof increases, certitude seems to decrease."[21] Again, as Newman will remind in the *Grammar*, certitude, as the issue of the "illative sense," is not the same as certainty. But unlike Kierkegaard, the Catholic spirit of Newman sees them compatible. He went the same length of belief as Kierkegaard without "leaping" because, without sacrificing the existential paradox, belief is not a leap at all but the recognition of accumulated probabilities expanded into the form of a fact.[22] Kierkegaardian distemper is a sign of the unbalanced reaction which frequently becomes the mode of inspired individuals fed up with the rationalist's abuse of reason, but who lack the Catholic balance which saves the reaction from becoming an irrational reactionism.

---

[20]Vid. Owen Chadwick, *The Popes and European Revolution* (Oxford: 1981), pp. 426-428.

[21]*Dread*, p. 125.

[22]John Coulson, *Religion and Imagination* (Oxford: 1981), p. 71.

Kierkegaard does recognize the facticity of the history in which Christian probabilities accumulate: "It is well known that Christianity is the only historical phenomenon which in spite of the historical, nay precisely by means of the historical, has offered itself to the individual as a point of departure for his eternal consciousness, has assumed to interest him in another sense than the merely historical, has proposed to base his eternal happiness on his relationship to something historical."[23] But any arbitrary historicism such as Liberal Protestantism would espouse, was as repugnant to his historicism as formal Idealism. The one fact of consequence is the historicity of Christ. Once that is established, all that is necessary is established. The Incarnation is the definitive lesson to be learned from history. And faith is the highest reach of subjectivity because it has the highest paradox as its object: ". . . the Eternal came into being at a definite moment in time as an individual man."[24]

Explanation of this historical economy involves what may be Kierkegaard's most complex and confusing category: Repetition, or *Gjentagelsen*. His attempt to simplify the term limps when he calls it a Platonic recollection "in a different direction," but that is how he describes it. Recollection is a retreat into an eternal world of ideas, or immortality; Repetition is a "forward-looking" recollection impelled by the absurd and which, in its fullest form, is eternity. It confronts a unified vision, fractures it, and then assembles a new unity incorporating the distinctions disclosed in the fractious analysis. Technically, Repetition is not exactly eschatological, for the "leap of faith" already has introduced the believer to an unfolding and eternal wholeness of existence. Repetition, however, does have to do with the future direction of Christian salvation already present in history. If we can associate it with proclaiming "the Lord's death until he comes" (1 Cor. 11:26) of which the sacrifice of Isaac is a type, and if it also

---

[23]*Fragments*, p. 92.
[24]*Postscript*, p. 152.

figures in Job's loss and gain, it may be that Repetition is Kierkegaard's groping form of the eucharistic *anamnesis*, the great Catholic "un-forgetting" next to which mere remembrance is banal, though the analogy is absent from the critical literature.

His whole treatment of the ecclesial dimension of existence is, at best, brittle. Extreme individualism has little place for the institutions of practical religion. Faith cannot pass from one soul to another, and the Church is nothing more for him than a maieutic in bringing each to his own faith. As Barth would come to question infant baptism, so Kierkegaard even doubts the propriety of the mass baptism by the apostles at Pentecost. But by the same token, this layman who abandoned the Lutheranism of his own state church, saw Protestant anthropology as the source of utilitarian moralizing and anthropomorphism which, respectively, would lead to Liberalism and Modernism, just as Newman saw in Liberalism the germ of atheism. Kierkegaard strongly rejected Luther's "faith alone"; in light of "double reflection," or reduplication of thought in existence, Luther's insistence on faith without works was totally repugnant and immoral. And without compromising his native loyalties, he found more evidence of the radical immolation of the self in the ancient Latin tradition than in what he knew of nordic Protestantism: "Yet still Catholicism has a conception and presentation of Christian identity . . . of becoming nothing in this world, whereas Protestantism is finiteness from end to end."[25]

In 1852, nearly all his reading was devoted to the Church Fathers, and Georg Brandes was certain that had he lived longer he would have made either "a leap into the black abyss of Catholicism, or over to the headland of freedom."[26] In a more psychoanalytical vein, Eric Pryzywara suspected that he was

---

[25]Søren Kierkegaard, "Eflerladte Papirer," 284, in Lowrie, op. cit., p. 523. Cf. ibid., p. 375. Kierkegaard's way of protesting against the complacency of the Danish state religion was hardly less bourgeois: he boycotted church services and spent Sunday mornings at his club.

[26]In Donald Nicholl, *Recent Thought in Focus* (London: 1952), p. 84.

longing for maternal consolation under the figures of the Blessed Virgin and the Church, though there is nothing pathological about that so long as mothers are meant to be, and so long as Our Lady and the Church are made to mother creation. On the subject of sceptics, in *Fear and Trembling* he can sound as stentorian as St. Pius X, for he says that objections to Christianity are not primarily from intellectual doubt but from insubordination and rebellion against all authority. The language is typical of an instinctive conservatism which made him a trusted friend of the King, Christian VIII, during the political unrest of 1846 and 1847, and a champion of apostolic succession in the Danish Church even when that Church was uninterested. The English Tractarians knew the feeling. Barth in his *No!* assumed that Kierkegaard was of Catholic sympathies concerning the "analogia entis." And Isaac Hecker, founder of the Society of St. Paul, was not the only reader to move from Kierkegaard to Catholicism, through the added influences of Pascal and Newman.

Two factors, however, militate against making him more Catholic than that. One is the extreme dualism of his dialectic. The other is the individualism of the inwardness theory (remembering that inwardness is but another term for subjectivity): "The Socratic secret, which must be preserved in Christianity, unless the latter is to be an infinite backward step, and which in Christ receives an intensification, by means of a more profound inwardness which makes it infinite, is that the movement of the spirit is inward, that the truth is the subject's transformation in himself."[27] Without an eschatological Kingdom, there are only two realities: the God-Man and the human soul. The incarnation is irrational and absurd to the human mind, but it is true because it is not absurd to the Divine. And because of that it is no longer absurd to man, either, because it bears a meaning for faith.

---

[27]*Postscript*, pp. 37f.

Then with Tertullian, Kierkegaard could affirm, "Credo quia absurdum est." He certainly does not believe because of the probability of propositions. All categories of objective knowledge vanish in the absolute presence of the holy. Aquinas hardly denied that, and indeed he lived it when propositions suddenly became so much straw in the face of theophany. But it can caricature theology to say as Jaroslav Pelikan says, and as Tyrrell objected against Newman's theory of development thereby marking his fated course from orthodoxy: once the Holy had become propositional, the object of intellectual apprehension, the God-Man relationship ceased being existential, the only dimension in which revelation and faith have any claim to meaning.[28] And so we are back again to subjectivity, and all the while respecting Kierkegaard's absolute insistence, that this subjectivity is not "personal distortion" as it is usually taken to mean, or the lack of certain truth. Subjectivity is personal appropriation. The subjective thinker is concerned only with what matters to him, bringing him to a deeper apprehension of reality. By circuitous routes from this concept would proceed an incongruous pair of developments: Barth's dialectical theology and Heidegger's own existentialism.

Subjectivity is the functional divider between philosophy and religion, the content of the second and third levels of perception mentioned above. Philosophy is the relation of intelligence to object; religion is the relation of subject to subject. The neo-Kantian protest against Hegelianism was this: any smudging of the distinction, any philosophical absorption of religion into philosophy itself becomes mystification. Kierkegaard's objection to Hegel was against the refusal to acknowledge the glory of an unknown God, and he argued his case with the tone of St. Paul before the sages of the Athenian academy.

---

[28]Cf. Jaroslav Pelikan, *Fools for Christ* (Philadelphia: 1955), p. 22; Sponheim, op. cit., p. 104.

So subjectivity is required of religion, and Maritain himself insists on it: "It is something to know that God is a transcendent and sovereign Self; but it is something else again to enter oneself and with all one's baggage — one's own existence and flesh and blood — into the vital relationship in which created subjectivity is brought face to face with this transcendent subjectivity and trembling and loving, looks to it for salvation. This is the business of religion."[29] But for the business to be honest, reason must be neither divinized nor destroyed. Rationalist religiosity ossifies the structures of belief, and Maritain could give a compact account of how that happens.[30] Natural law becomes Grotius's geometric pattern of culture; the good of the soul becomes Descartes's angelism; divine omniscience and redemption become Leibniz's logicism and optimism; the universal divine causality becomes Spinoza's monism; supernatural infused knowledge turns into Berkeley's metaphysical idealism; the divine moral law passes through Kant as ethical purism; eschatology changes gears as Hegel's evolutionism; and the apocalyptic New Jerusalem broods as Marx's evolutionary state.

But an alternative to all this was the way of irrationalism, a corruption of philosophy and a torment of religion leading to the highly refined wildness of Bohme, Jacobi, Nietzsche, Chekov, and, it may be said as Maritain indeed does say, the "knight of faith" Kierkegaard. Its most degenerate hybrids today may be the "New Age" cults with their gnostic anthropology and romantic naturalism. For recognizing a need to sacrifice the intellect, they obliterate it instead.

Kierkegaard never reconciled Holy Love and Absolute Otherness. He managed only to affirm that "man dies to his entire immediacy" in order to assimilate to the infinite Whole. The quality of such existence itself is paradoxical, a synthesis of

---

[29]Jacques Maritain, *Challenges and Renewals* (Notre Dame, Ind.: 1966), p. 67.
[30]Ibid., pp. 108-109.

the infinite and finite, of the eternal and temporal. Since neither speculation nor systematization can serve the paradox, "existential thinking" is the only way to analyze the qualitative dialectic of being. The essence of existential thought is dialectic and paradox. And it is by having given the world this analysis that Kierkegaard has been called the Father of Existentialism. His biographer Lowrie rather would call him not even the Grandfather but something of a Great Uncle; James Brown contends that he is not an existentialist at all, if existentialism means a method whose basic premise is its subjective attitude and not the desire for a theological conclusion. Modern existentialism follows a line from Kierkegaard but reaches various conclusions alien to him: Heidegger's non-theism, Sartre's atheism, Jasper's ambiguity. Kierkegaard acknowledges that an understanding of man, nature and God is not derived directly from the dialectic of existence any more than from the dialectic of reason. To say other would be to commit an immanenist denial of the paradox of Christianity itself. Kierkegaard's contribution to Christian thought has been to show the deficiencies in Hegelianism while positing a special kind of personalism by perceiving reality as both existence and idea.[31]

Contrasting the superiority of the individual human being to the being of natural objects, existentialism can guide a Protestant Kierkegaard, a Catholic Marcel, a Jewish Buber and an Orthodox Berdyaev.[32] Pascal could join the list for choosing the God of Abraham over the God of the *Philosophes*; and Augustine, too, could qualify, if only for declaring from the start of the *Confessions*: "Thou hast formed us for thyself, and our hearts are restless till they find their rest in thee." Inasmuch as, for each of them, man "makes himself" by interiorizing the gift of God, none is like the modern existentialist for whom man comes into fulfillment by "creating value" for himself.[33]

---

[31]Brown, op. cit., pp. 62-63.

[32]Macquarrie, *An Existentialist Theology*, op. cit., p. 16.

[33]Brown, op. cit., p. 101.

The modern existentialist is an atheist whose attempts at human autonomy have moved man into an anxiety unthinkable to Kierkegaard in his own dread at the prospect of nothingness. The anxiety of the newer existentialism has been the anguish of man actually desirous of nothingness and still forced to exist in spite of himself. But this idea did not spring fresh from the head of any modern Zeus. It was the culmination of the first rumblings of an earlier departure from reason, perfectly Thomistic in the primary it gave to existence, *existentia ut exercita*, yet, as Maritain reminded his own generation, contemptuous of essences in its theory of subjectivity.

Modern existentialism is what is left of Kierkegaard's sense of the nothingness of the creature, once the Creator has been neglected. It is what Kierkegaard feared would cause chaos: the deadly confusion of paradox and nonsense. Both existentialisms, theist and atheist, have their spiritual import, and it may require the Scholastic prudence of one as rare as Maritain to discern them: "For the first it would be the mystical experience of apophatic theology in which God is known as unknown and which Existentialist philosophy misconstrues, pilfering it all the while from the saints. For the second kind of Existentialist it would be the mystical knowledge of Hell."[34]

---

[34]Maritain, *Range of Reason*, op. cit., p. 46.

Newman on Assent
to Religious Belief

Sources for a System

Immanuel Kant wrote no hymns, and John Henry Newman (1801-1890) in one sense wrote nothing but hymns. There, for the hasty, is the difference between the two. Though the critical method of neither yields to the other in architecture, the granite of Kant's categorical imperative is solid and silent when set against the lyrical fabric of Newman's "illative sense," a term he did not coin but which he grafted onto common thought. If stones could sing they would take their pitch from what Newman wrote in *An Essay in Aid of a Grammar of Assent*. The title itself is hymnodic and of a personality unlike the Kantian which defined sacred speech as unreliable speech. Newman was not overly serious about his own contribution, nor did he weigh it gravely against other attentions. He delayed its composition to pen, among other works, the *Apologia* in roughly the number of days Handel took to write *Messiah*, and with the same consuming passion. Then it was back to the understated meter of the *Grammar* and its quiet doctrine of sober words about holy things. An inspired Newmanism in one of the *University Sermons* would surely have annoyed Kant: "Half the controversies in the world are verbal ones and, could they be brought to plain issue, they would be brought to a prompt determination."[1]

---

[1]John Henry Newman, *Fifteen Sermons Preached Before the University of Oxford* (London: 1871, orig. 1843), p. 192, hereafter *US*.

Newman allows himself to be called a philosopher and theologian only as such serve the cure of souls, and his method is of a thinker whose writings are all to a purpose, and a pastoral purpose at that. When still in his twenties, he is "a Tutor, a Parish Priest and a Fellow."[2] When dedicating the *Grammar* in 1870, he is neither Tutor nor Fellow, but still much a parish priest. The pastoral function is not to invent words but to explain them. As Kant was as much a philosopher as Newman could not think himself to be, it is logical that the Kantian theory of knowledge should register exasperation at the rational limits of religion which were an inspiration to Newman. The genius of Kant had moved the gears of a mental revolution by considering truth in relation to the individual; this had been the definitive split from older rationalism. By considering truth in relation to the whole personality, Newman's genius began a less boisterous revolution, though one more vital for the modern intelligence of calamitous confrontation with social alienation and collectivism.

The author of the *Grammar* does not demur from quoting himself frequently as a prouder man might, and he goes back some thirty years to an essay of 1841 to make a pivotal point: "The heart is commonly reached not through the reason but through the imagination, by means of direct impression, by the testimony of facts and events, by history, by description. Persons influence us, voices melt us, looks subdue us, deeds inflame us."[3] His purpose is no less psychological than epistemological; and part of his plan is to eradicate any false chasm between the two. The two must mean something to each other simply because the Incarnation of Jesus Christ is not gratuitous; it is essential to a sensible account of the universe, uniting the deepest meaning of death understood as a physical ending, with happiness as the metaphysical end of it. The conclusion of the *Grammar* had been

---

[2]*The Letters and Diaries of John Henry Newman*, ed. by Charles Stephen Dessain (London: 1961-), 7 Sept. 1829, hereafter *LD*.

[3]John Henry Newman, *An Essay in Aid of a Grammar of Assent* (Westminster, Md.: 1973, orig. 1870), pp. 92-93, hereafter *Grammar*.

known from the start: the central doctrine of revelation, the mediation of Christ, becomes the remedy for the sense of sin. That sense can be recognized, but not resolved, by natural religion. It is "no dreary matter of antiquarianism; we do not contemplate it in conclusions drawn from dumb documents and dead events, but by faith exercised in ever-living objects, and by the appropriation and use of ever-recurring gifts."[4] Newman then sets out upon a contemplation of the holiest "in the height and in the depth" undeterred by the limits which reason had placed on certitude in the Kantian system. There unfolds in the pages of the *Grammar* a complex picture of the reason conditioned by time and events, and animated beyond Kant's valiant attempt to improve the isolated aridities of rationalism and Idealism alike.

The project could be done in philosophic hymnody and hymnodic philosophy by virtue of Newman's sources in some of his preliminary writings on the imagination. The *Grammar* explains how the authenticity of religious belief depends on its credibility to the imagination in which it originates; but to do this, it has to rally language with a force adequate to the message. This was not an easy task, as Newman's vocabulary was far more pragmatic than philosophical.

The role of conscience over and above system may have come from Kant to Newman through an array of channels, but Kant himself was an inchoate, though not anonymous, figure to him. Deliberately did he leave uncut half the pages of Kant's *Critique* in his Meiklejohn translation: "I do not think I am bound to read them (the German Idealists) . . . for notoriously they have come to no conclusion."[5] The *Grammar's* use of such

---

[4]Ibid., p. 487.

[5]Vid. Edwin Sillem, "General Introduction to the Study of Newman's Philosophy" in *The Philosophical Notebook of John Henry Newman* (Louvain: 1969), Vol. I, p. 229. While Bremond has done violence to Newman by trying to turn him into a neo-Kantian, he also errs when he claims that Newman was almost wholly ignorant of German criticism.

terms as nature, moral sense, and moral perception, was common to the British empiricism of the day. The focus of interest at the time was overwhelmingly epistemological. Newman makes no apologies for an impreciseness. The *Grammar* really is an attempt at some modest systematic for what had developed out of his pulpit rhetoric, as that was the foundation of his intellectual life, and any rhetoric is by its nature hostile to methodical vivisection. A sermon is the platform in fact for a key to his code in the *Grammar*: "Moral character in itself, whether good or bad, as exhibited in thought and conduct, surely cannot be duly represented in words." Of language it is at most a defect, and not a fault, that it only does what it should; speech is, after all, "an artificial system and adapted for particular purposes, which have been determined by our wants."[6]

The statement, evidence of its own thesis, was essential to the empiricists among whom Newman is spotlighted for the audience of the ages. But empiricist is hardly a fair definition, given the varieties of empiricism and their own complicated sources. We know how Descartes imputed to the mind the character of being with more certitude than he gave the body; Kant called that problematic Idealism. When the world is hypothetical, hypotheses about it will become the world's one industry. And so it commandeered the fertile mind of Locke to whom Newman expresses profound scientific and moral respect.[7] Now, Locke posited the ability of perceptions to represent bodies. That was one theory. But there was also the more

---

And Sillem (ibid., pp. 228-240) effectively refutes Pattison who says "the grand development of human reason from Aristotle down to Hegel was a sealed book to him." Cf. Henry Bremond, *The Mystery of Newman* (London: 1907), pp. 78-79; Mark Pattison, *Essays* (London: 1889), Vol. II, pp. 210-211. Any Kantian ghost is banished by Newman's incantation: "We reason in order to enlarge our knowledge of matters, which do not depend on us for being what they are." (*Grammar*, p. 222).

[6]*US*, p. 71.

[7]Cf. eg., *Grammar*, p. 162.

dogmatic Idealism of Berkeley for whom nothing exists outside the mind. And there was the definitive empiricism of Hume who denied any objective view of the world, and offered no accessible explanation for the roots of our own impressions of it.

The empiricist moves from a recollection of the Psalmist's awe at God's mindfulness of man, to the perplexity of Job in his moral isolation. But inasmuch as Job resolved the matter through faith, he parts with the empiricist who moves into another mode of resolution more contemporary in feeling, that of perpetual anxiety. Hume asks, "Where am I, or what? From what causes do I derive my existence, and to what conditions shall I return?"[8] Much of Newman's attractiveness shines from his sensitivity to that suffused alarm, as he measures the pulse of a post-Idealist generation which he says gropes in an unprecedented kind of darkness. Newman's final rejection of Hume came not because he differed with Hume's judgment apart from the apparatus of Christian belief. J. M. Cameron put it happily in saying that the difference was more one of psychological depth, with Hume confined to *l'esprit de géometrie* as Newman exulted in *l'esprit de finesse*.[9]

The *Grammar* became the model of an effective Christian address to an alienated culture in language aware of its condition, in a manner aware of what it was confronting. Newman would open the empiricist's eyes to a remedy for his confusion which did not cancel empiricism but warned of wrong issue. For the empiricist is not all ivory tower. And when he seems so, he is even then quite capable of giving a perfectly mathematical account of the tower. Even Berkeley allows that

---

[8]David Hume, *A Treatise of Human Nature* (Oxford: 1896), p. 269. Cf. *Grammar*, p. 80.

[9]J. M. Cameron, "Newman and the Empiricist Tradition" in *The Rediscovery of Newman: An Oxford Symposium*, ed. John Coulson and A. M. Allchin (London: 1967), p. 94, hereafter "NET."

exploration of any number of hypotheticals will not alter a fact.[10] And Hume admits as possible anything conceivable and then slams down on miracles as though swatting a fly. Newman was not too timid to enjoy Socratic ironies in solid empiricist good humor. Often the irony is none too subtle and the *Grammar* is an open field for his wit. Odd, then, that some should say he wrote it in weariness. It may be among the wittiest of his works, however perverse that may seem after a superficial reading.

When writing normally was a "pain and grief" to him, there must have been a glint in his eye when he sketched the statesman who fancied Demerara was an island, and acknowledged the Anglo-Saxon attitude toward the frog-eating French, and remarked the mistaken belief that Joanna Southcote was a messenger from heaven. And there is the nice gossip about the prodigy who could give the names on all the shops from Hyde Park Corner to the Bank, and another who recited the academical history of any Oxford M. S. at random. Here is a chance to slice at the conceit that Newman was a melancholy man. Baron von Hügel (1852-1925) was a chief instrument in spreading this report, which contradicts so many other contemporaries, but in that case Henry Tristram gave a good reply: "... if von Hügel found Newman depressing, it was due in part to the effect that von Hügel had on Newman."[11] The *Grammar* is grand mental adventure, but one which does find home. There could be no mind more domestic, as distinct from pedantic, and his journey did "not ask to see the distant scene," though it was confident that there was one.

The sobriety and practicality of the empiricists, with their totally experientialist approach, made more efficient the

[10]George Berkeley, *The Principles of Human Knowledge* in *The Works of George Berkeley, Bishop of Cloyne*, Vol. II, ed. A. A. Luce and T. E. Jessop (London: 1949), p. 42.

[11]Henry Tristram in *The Dublin Review* (Autumn 1966), p. 300 (paper originally read to the Newman Conference at Beaumont, 1945). Vid. also *Grammar*, pp. 33, 198, 295, 340-341.

development of the historical method and of social anthropology. That was one reason for Voltaire's preference for Locke to the Cartesians. Both sciences figure repeatedly in Newman's speculations and receive from him a protection not typical of many other Christian apologists in that age. Doubtless, he could not have felt comfortable at anything like the debate between Samuel Wilberforce and Thomas Huxley, which was an elevated anticipation of the Scopes trial. And he was incapable of Keble's spectacularly ludicrous fossil theory (that if they were in the rocks, God put them there). The experientialism of the empiricists, however different their conclusions, did commend itself to the affinity of personality and method in Newman's own mind. His recourse to Pascal is typical of this.[12]

If we might be allowed the expression, attention to social experience and inner conscience developed through the Newman synthesis into a psychology of history. That is, he created a systematic of the role of interior perception as an historical evidence of the one true God who is perceived by different people in different times and places. Study of the Arian heresy had been the efficient cause of his own conversion. Or it might better be called an "arrival," as he said his conversion was a matter of coming into port. The Arian drama had been high intellectual theory, no less for the nineteenth century don who read about it than for the fourth century controversialists who lived it. It was anything but the autonomous invention of theory; it was nothing if it was not the influential torrent of personalities and events whose stories flooded upon themselves. Because history is kinetic, Newman respected its power to lead him some place, quite as Harnack, of whom we shall later read, thought it static and for that reason tried to lead it to a conclusion he had already made for it. "Christianity is a history supernatural, and

---

[12]Cf. John Henry Newman, *Apologia pro Vita Sua* (London: 1890, orig. 1864), p. 200, hereafter *Apologia*; *Letters and Correspondence of John Henry Newman During his Life in the English Church*, ed. Anne Mozley (London: 1898, orig. 1891), Vol. II, p. 307.

almost scenic: it tells us what its Author is, by telling us what he
has done."[13]

Though times had changed, the economy of perception had
not, and sixteen hundred centuries and more had not made its
defect any less dolorous. Newman is intolerant of any
epistemology which deals loosely with historical reality and its
significant impression on the conscience. His certainty on the
matter parts him from the Liberals at once, and becomes a
paradigm for the whole play between history sacred and secular:
"Let the Church be removed, and the world will soon come to its
end."[14] The rationalizations which Gibbon had proposed to
explain away the fruitfulness of Christian institutions, are
rejected by Newman for having ignored the motive behind the
early Christians' real assent to a thing "in the unseen, not in the
obsolete."[15]

Without recourse to the *Grammar* as a whole, and especially
upon cursory encounter with its fifth chapter on apprehension
and assent in religion, Newman's vote for Christianity can sound
very Kantian indeed in its moral representation of "only one
religion in the world which tends to fulfill the aspirations, needs
and foreshadowings of natural faith and devotion . . ."; and he
can seem then to lapse into a defensive syllogism when he
decides ". . . either Christianity is from God or a revelation has
yet to be given to us."[16] Yet the argument is not so brusque as
some would contend.[17] For example, having challenged the
reader to doubt whether the Christian claim can possibly be
rejected by reason functioning properly, he explains: "Many

---

[13]*Grammar*, p. 96.

[14]John Henry Newman, *An Essay on the Development of Christian
Doctrine* (Westminster, Md.: 1968, orig. 1845), p. 204, hereafter
Development. Cf. "NET," p. 94.

[15]*Grammar*, p. 487; cf. pp. 462ff.

[16]Ibid., p. 430; cf. p. 308.

[17]Cf. eg., Christopher Hollis, *Newman and the Modern World*
(London: 1967), p. 171, hereafter *NMW*.

have been converted and sustained in their faith by this argument, which admits of being powerfully stated; but still such statement is after all only intended to be a vehicle of thought, and to open the mind to the apprehension of the facts of the case, and to trace them and their implications in outline, not to convince them by the logic of its mere wording."[18]

In the final reckoning, there is no point in making a case for Christianity with minds that do not even accept the premises of natural religion, "not as claiming any right to be impatient or peremptory with any one, but because it is plainly absurd to attempt to prove a second proposition to those who do not admit the first."[19] And then, in distancing himself from the naturalism of such as Paley, he also disallows any phenomenal interpretation which had no place for an "inwardness" of faith.

As his last major work, the *Grammar* is to Newman as public a confession of mature principles as *Religion Within the Limits of Reason Alone* is to Kant. And while their interests and ends were hardly sympathetic, both used these studies to move beyond the bankrupt confidences of astringent rationalism and complacent empiricism in their manufacture of reliable frameworks for belief and judgment. The gauntlet was thrown down before the Liberal materialists who were the closest in Newman's time to the spiritually autistic secularists of the present moment who think it is possible to be "post-Christian." Again, he draws upon his *Tamworth Reading Room* material, a coruscating series which defined the heart of his contrast between what he will call notional and real assents:

> People will say to me, that it is but a dream to suppose that Christianity should regain the organic power in human society which once it possessed. I cannot help that; I never said it could. I am not a politician; I am proposing no measures, but exposing a fallacy and resisting a pretence. Let Benthamism reign, if men have no aspirations; but do

---

[18]*Grammar*, p. 309.
[19]Ibid., p. 416.

not tell them to be romantic and then solace them with
"glory": do not attempt by philosophy what once was done
by religion. The ascendancy of faith may be impracticable,
but the reign of knowledge is incomprehensible. The
problem for statesmen of this age is how to educate the
masses, and literature and science cannot give the
solution.[20]

It was a challenge and was meant to be one. Christianity
would need a new apologetic for a new culture, but it did not
need to be apologized for. Contrition was rather due from those
who exploited history as a subjective artifact to justify their
private prejudices. As Hegel and Marx would exploit the whole
motion and motive of history, so had the Enlightenment
exploited the Christian experience, and Gibbon as its exemplar
becomes a model of guilt. A serene aphorism rises against any
such inference: "Many a man will live and die upon a dogma; no
man will be a martyr for a conclusion."[21]

Conclusions are not other than opinions. A religion
founded on such premises is a "literary religion" of calculations,
which does not commit the person to realities. Dogma fills
history with wet martyrs who shed their blood and dry martyrs
who shed their egos; the dearth of dogma breeds damp martyrs,
those speculating dilettantes who shed everything but their blood
and egos. It is Newman's project to explain that definitive
realities are revealed in revelations. Reason alone cannot
motivate the personality to accountability in experience, nor can
it alone make the personality accountable to the judgments of
experience: ". . . no religion yet has been a religion of physics or
of philosophy. It has ever been synonymous with revelation. It
never has been a deduction from what we know; it has ever been
a message, a history, or a vision. No legislator or priest ever
dreamed of educating our moral nature by science or by

---

[20]Ibid., p. 92.
[21]Ibid., p. 93.

argument."[22] The Kantian amalgamation of empirical realism and transcendental Idealism gave the same account, but resolved that because such was the case, the case was regrettable. Logic, then, could have nothing more to say in the categories of revelation. In counterpoint, Newman made it his reason for saying so much.

Nothing in the Newman literature discounts natural evidence for belief; but inasmuch as he held that revelation is received by a self-authenticating impression, natural evidence cannot be sufficient for proof. Here is one example of how historical awareness moved him to animate empiricist individualism until it became a form of personalism, not as Liberalism would make it a subjectivist autonomy, the antique tyranny of the ego, but as the vital engagement of the whole moral personality. Sir Robert Peel assumed as axiomatic that a mind once acquainted with the latest discoveries in experimental science should have "more enlarged conceptions of God's providence, and a higher reverence for His Name."[23] But as far as Newman is concerned, such is true only of religious minds; it is paradoxical in the irreligious and settles nothing. He points a finger at insecure apologists, the vacuous pawns of human respect whom a later vulgarism would come to call trendy; they try to "defend" Christianity by making metaphysics a gloss on physics, and under intimidation from technocracy try to make of each new assertion of theoretical physics a direct statement of theology. Led by public opinion and anxious for preferred emoluments, they "from a nervous impatience lest Scripture should for one moment seem inconsistent with the results of some speculation of the hour, are for ever proposing geological or ethnological comments upon it, which they have to alter or obliterate before the work is well dry, from changes in the

---

[22]Ibid., p. 96.
[23]Ibid., p. 94.

progressive science, which they have so efficaciously brought to its aid."[24]

His own evidences for religious belief were born directly of a fertile imagination which he spent a lifetime examining with utter fascination, as in the *Apologia*: "I used to wish the Arabian tales were true: my imagination ran on unknown influences, on magical powers, and talismans ... I thought life might be a dream, or I an Angel, and all this world a deception, my fellow-angels by a playful device concealing themselves from me, and deceiving me with the semblance of a material world."[25] This was the phenomenon, the imaginative faculty with its impressions, that might shed light on the nature of belief and its object. And so he wonders in empiricist diction what the phenomena of the external world might be other than a "divine mode" of conveying reality to the mind, and the influence of "being on being."

Newman's place in the empiricist tradition is singular as he brings to it a particular poetry in the critique of consciousness. And though, to say the least, it is misleading to identify sacramentalism with Idealist metaphysics, his cautious appropriation of the empiricist sense of the self becomes an excuse for Mark Pattison to lump sacerdotalism with Kantianism in a kind of mish-mash; but it is a significant contrast to Mill's empiricism and nominalism which to Newman's regret overwhelmed Oxford after his departure in 1845. He means that the particular empiricist bias for the conscience, be it rooted in Kant or whomever, when once discarded would but surrender the field to the implacable utilitarians and secularists. Those who have accused Newman of opening the way to Modernism by a Humean scepticism imputed to him, argue in the same line. Those who have admired him for paving the Modernist path merely gloss the same fantasy with optimism. But the Humean scepticism was about the capacity of the mind to perceive truth;

---

[24]John Henry Newman, *The Idea of a University Defined and Illustrated* (Westminster, Md.: 1973, orig. 1873), p. 472, hereafter *Idea*.

[25]*Apologia*, p. 16.

Newman's is rather a scepticism about the capacity of civilization to keep the perception. He rejects Locke's concept of "degrees" of assent since "we might as well talk of degrees of truth as of degrees of assent."[26] But he knows there are degrees of opinion, and that these fluctuate in a culture; if they are not stabilized by the illative sense, they will become the calamity of culture. Future social engineers would fail to heed his warning that "the lowest class, which is most numerous, and is infidel, will rise up from the depths of the modern cities, and will be the new scourge of God."[27]

However complex may be the developing maze of empiricism and Idealism, the important thing is that Newman begins as they do, with the interior impression. A characteristic contribution is that pastoral *animus* which draws from empiricism its fascination for the commonplace and makes it a canon of his comparatively unsystematic style (which attains to a system certainly more in the *Grammar* than in the *Essay on the Development of Christian Doctrine*). The result is a near Chestertonian fascination for the mystery discerned in ordinary things. Newman had the singular acumen to bring the mystery to a resolution without losing its paradox.

It may well be that much of Newman's strength as a theologian is located in his remove from Idealist metaphysics. Empiricism is bankrupt for denying that informative statements are analytic and conversely that analytic statements are not informative in any important sense (a problem Kant partially tried to address in his theory of *a priori* synthetic judgment); and Newman's acquaintance with it distinguished his ability to construct an epistemology enticing to Catholic and non-Catholic alike. But empiricism also helped to save him from the fatal confusion of philosophy and theology. Having scouted the domain of philosophy and the confines of its attentions, he was

---

[26]*Grammar*, pp. 173ff.
[27]*LD*, XXV, p. 337.

not tempted to lop and lame revelation to fit it. Philosophy is valid as a method to verify belief; it is useless and disordered as a method for constructing belief. Hence the *Grammar*, by a respect for conscience no less than Kant's, becomes a *riposte* to the Kantian conclusions and might be called *Reason Within the Limits of Religion Alone*. If Kant presumed upon theologians as a philosopher, Newman would not mirror the mistake.

> It is notorious how ridiculous a clever man may make himself, who ventures to argue with professed theologians, critics, or geologists, though without positive defects in knowledge of his subject. Priestley, great in electricity and chemistry, was but a poor ecclesiastical historian. The Author of the Minute Philosopher is also the Author of the Analyst. Newton wrote not only his "Principia," but his comments on the Apocalypse; Cromwell, whose actions savoured of the boldest logic, was a confused speaker. In these, and various similar instances, the defect lay, not so much in an ignorance of facts, as in an inability to handle these facts suitably; in feeble or perverse modes of abstraction, observation, comparison, analysis, inference, which nothing could have obviated, but that which was wanting, — a specific talent, and a ready exercise of it.[28]

More specifically, Newman's neglect of Idealism ensured that he would not capitulate to philosophy as the umpire and referee in theological discourse, as Coleridge (1772-1834) succumbed, or to surrender to the "insatiable appetite of philosophy to make a meal of all things, the sacred science of theology included."[29] The temptation of course was great, especially in any approach to a concept so ephemeral in vernacular use as conscience. Hence Coleridge's bizarre and ever fashionable confession that "he should have been a Christian had Christ never lived; that all that was good in the teaching of Christ was to be found in Plato, in Zoroaster,

---

[28]*Grammar*, p. 340.
[29]"NET," p. 96.

Confucius and the Gymnosophists . . ."[30] It is not hard to see why Coleridge has been accused of using Kantian expression to disguise Platonism. In an article of 1838 on "The Prospects of the Anglican Church," Newman had described Coleridge as a "very original thinker who, while he indulged a liberty of speculation which no Christian can tolerate, and advanced conclusions which were often heathen rather than Christian, yet after all instilled a higher philosophy into inquiring minds, than they had hitherto been accustomed to accept."[31] The prudential balance here, a dynamic where Coleridge afforded only a fluidity, is another testimony to his practice of measured judgment, or of the Aristotelian mean of "phronesis," to which he makes explicit recourse again and again.[32] Above all, it retires, to the satisfaction of all save those resurrectionists who disinter decayed ideas as substitutes for the risen Christ, the notion of Newman as a subjectivist. "Duties change, but truths never."[33] Thus, the way "men differ so widely from each other in religion and moral perceptions" only makes more wonderful the objectivity of truth.[34]

Metaphor and Imagination

Newman's *Idea of a University* is a high flowering of how he would assert the limits of language in any religious project. The archetypal controversialist disdained controversy for controversy's sake; such would be a disputatiousness worthy of his subject. And when language had to be rallied to his cause, he spared no effort to depict a faith which in its final definition

[30]Hugh Fausset, *Samuel Taylor Coleridge* (London: 1926), p. 311.
[31]John Henry Newman, *Essays Critical and Historical* (London: 1897, orig. 1871), p. 268.
[32]Cf. eg., *Grammar*, pp. 354ff.
[33]*US*, p. 193.
[34]*Grammar*, p. 358.

cannot be argued for at all. Language can only display the difference between faith and the rival systems of intuition, and these men are left to decide for themselves: "We need not dispute, we need not prove, we need but define."[35]

Thus without jeopardizing the principle of objectivity, the *Grammar* goes beyond the empiricism of the day to an almost Kierkegaardian existentialist critique of judgment and belief, while remaining absorbed in the philosophy of language. Hume was "this acute, though most low-minded of speculators."[36] Low-minded possibly because of what does seem, in comparison with Newman's other references, an aggravating glibness in logical analysis. Yet his early philosophical expressions reek of Hume, though even more of Bishop Butler, to whom he gives first place among English philosophers. And he writes in a paper he chose not to publish: "In most departments of writing to speak of self is egotistical; not so in metaphysics. In it the writer cannot propose to do more than record his own opinions, the phenomena to which he appeals and the principles which he assumes being within his own breast . . ."[37]

If at the time he lacked "confidence enough" for publication,[38] confidence came with the *Grammar*, for there he writes:

> I begin with expressing a sentiment which is habitually in my thoughts, whenever they are turned to the subject of mental or moral science, and which I am as willing to apply here to the Evidences of Religion as it properly applies to Metaphysics or Ethics, viz. that in these provinces of inquiry egotism is true modesty. In religious inquiry each of us can speak only for himself, and for himself he has a right to speak. His own experiences are enough for himself, but he cannot speak for others: he cannot lay down the law; he can

---

[35]Ibid., p. 293.

[36]*Idea*, p. 31.

[37]1 Dec., 1859, in unpublished papers at the Birmingham Oratory; vid. J. M. Cameron, *The Night Battle* (London: 1962), p. 221.

[38]Cf. *Philosophical Papers*, Birmingham Oratory, Sundries: A. 46. 3.

only bring his own experiences to the common stock of psychological facts.[39]

None of these facts could obtain without the imagination, by which Newman certainly means more than an ability to visualize in the abstract, or a mechanical sense perception which gives a novel intuition of reality. His concept of it is formed most particularly by Coleridge, and means the stimulation of a structured feeling. The imagination remains unpredictable as a mental faculty distinct from the reality it perceives; Newman, after all, is not an Idealist. Coleridge conceded to the imagination a power which "dissolves, diffuses, dissipates, in order to re-create."[40] And in this uncertainty of result lies the puzzlement which the imagination presents to philosophy. Wordsworth had been so struck by Coleridge's theory that he abandoned his clockwork idea of the mind and eventually paid tribute to the imagination in the first major philosophical poem in English, "The Prelude." No longer could one patronize the imagination as a fanciful idiosyncrasy: Coleridge had exposed the "living and prime agent" of perception. As agent it comes in two parts, the primary one being God's "eternal act of creation" and the second being human literary imagination which becomes the expression of the first. By actualizing, combining, and humanizing the most important human matters, language conducts human impressions to certitude. Coleridge's own grammar, or analytic, of assent in *Aids to Reflection* passes

---

[39]*Grammar*, p. 384.

[40]Samuel Taylor Coleridge, *Biographia Literaria* (London: 1952, orig., 1817), chap. XIII; vid. John Coulson, *Religion and Imagination* (Oxford: 1981), p. 7, hereafter *RI*. Charles Frederick Harrold quite incredibly claims that Coleridge had absolutely no influence on Newman whose "own theory of knowledge and faith was fully outlined" by 1835; the same author exaggerates Newman's much later familiarity with the Kantian literature and claims that Kant was an important positive influence. Cf. Harrold, *John Henry Newman* (London: 1945), pp. 135ff.

through theological refinements into the shape of Newman's "grammar" of how certitude is established. The substantial Coleridge thesis is Doric in its sturdy confidence: "To believe and understand are not diverse things, but the same thing in different periods of growth."[41]

In the same economy, faith and belief are different but co-relative in a process of gestation, the one is the nascent shape of the other. This is the basic concept explained in Newman's critique of assents. As the evidence of God eludes empirically verifiable evidence, certain knowledge of him does not have to be attended by clear knowledge; Newman asserts this in the distinction between certitude as a mental state and certainty as a quality of propositions.[42] If the distinctions seem dangerously subtle, they are a challenge to the particular modern supinity of thought which sentimentalizes religious intuition until belief is exclusively a matter of "feeling." Metaphor as the vehicle of certitude becomes the primary mode of language for Newman, and literal or discursive speech is secondary and abstracted. And consequently, as faith grows into belief it assumes new speech, new "organons" (the term is Coleridge's) which identify the Church as a linguistic community. This is totally out of sorts with Kant's void ecclesiology, and the antithesis of Hume's doctrine of poetry as misrepresentation, but it would find a friendly corroboration in Chesterton's aphorism: "The aim of good prose words is to mean what they say. The aim of good poetical words is to mean what they do not say."[43]

Assent indicates the commitment of the whole person, in bodily sense and soul. Newman was incapable of dualist conceits, as his long disparagement of the novatians attests.[44] In this lies

---

[41]Samuel Taylor Coleridge, *Aids to Reflection* (London: 1904, orig. 1825), p. 128.

[42]*Grammar*, p. 344.

[43]G. K. Chesterton, "Daily News" column, 22 April 1905.

[44]Cf. John Henry Newman, *Parochial and Plain Sermons* (London: 1891-1896, orig. 1834-1843), Vol. IV, p. 325.

the certification of the truth of religious experience, for it is not otherwise evident how the attachment of imagination to belief makes it valid. Newman insists that a thing must be proved to be both true and certain before it can properly be believed. In the case of a belief in something which cannot be explained, the appeal must be to the imagination. And this requires, not certitude or religious belief at all to begin; an assumption, or assent, is needed, and its certainty in turn leads to a higher certitude.

A hard question is asked of belief: is it possible to rise from a "dreamy acquiescence in an abstract truth" to recognize "the duty of giving it practical expression?"[45] The saint is the salutary evidence of the possibility. Fanatics and demagogues have believed, too, but saints provide the exemplary means of distinguishing between merely formal agreement to an idea and the decision to act upon a fact, moving from notion to real assent. And, parenthetically, on such a distinction does the Church make her own designation of martyrs apart from others who commit themselves, even mortally, to false causes.

> If, on the other hand, we would see what the force of simple assent can be, viewed apart from its reflex confirmation, we have but to look at the generous and uncalculating energy of faith as exemplified in the primitive Martyrs, in the youths who defied the pagan tyrant, or the maidens who were silent under his tortures. It is assent, pure and simple, which is the motive cause of great achievements; it is a confidence, growing out of instincts rather than arguments, stayed upon a vivid apprehension, and animated by a transcendent logic, more concentrated in will and in deed for the very reason that it has not been subjected to any intellectual development.[46]

---

[45]*Grammar*, p. 78. Cf. ibid., pp. 63, 67.
[46]Ibid., p. 216.

Newman thus provides evidence of his basic procedure for verifying the object of belief: the assent teaches the grammar.[47] Belief is initiated and doubt flees; the job of the analyst is to explain why this ballet of transferals has occurred. Newman is nothing if not consistent in rallying reason for defining faith as an act. Faith is not a prejudice; it is not prejudice in ordinary intellects or in extraordinary intellects. And so one can well decide that Newman intended the *Grammar* less as a philosophical treatise on belief and imagination than as an argument for how the amateur has as much claim to certitude as does the expert theologian, an item quite in keeping with the challenge of Coleridge and Wordsworth to erudite empiricists for whom religious certitude meant "the want of imagination."[48] Belief, then, is not dismissible as a gratuitous "leap of faith," for while it may seem so from the start, it is not so in retrospect when feet have been set firmly on an accumulation of probabilities. Newman had touched on this in an early sermon, "The Influence of Natural and Revealed Religion Respectively," and only later discovered Coleridge's *Biographia Literaria* which contains similar expressions.[49] The difference between Newman and Kierkegaard on the matter of probabilities may well amount, as Coulson would have it, to no more than that between retrospective and prospective ways of looking at the same fact: it is spoken of as a "leap" *before*, and is only *afterward* perceived as a polygon expanding into a circle.[50]

---

[47]*RI*, p. 71.
[48]Ibid., p. 9.
[49]Cf. H. F. Davis, "Was Newman a Disciple of Coleridge?" in *The Dublin Review* (October 1945); *US*, Sermon 7.
[50]*RI*, p. 71.

Defining His Terms

In pursuit of his points, Newman uses a basic vocabulary well within the reach of the reader of the day. Sometimes his terms can lead to ambiguity. This is, after all, only "an essay in aid of a grammar." But he does define them. "Apprehension," which he prefers to "understanding" as it is idiomatically used, is an intelligent acceptance of the idea or fact presented by a proposition.[51] "Notional assent" is the absolute and unconditional acceptance of the proposition of an idea.[52] "Real assent" is the absolute and unconditional acceptance of a fact.[53] Real and notional assents are sometimes thought roughly to match the relationship between intelligence and reason in Aquinas. For Aquinas, however, observation and the discursive use of reason should prepare the way for the intellect's grasp of the quiddity of things; Newman's theory of real and notional assent often parallels the Thomistic scheme, but — influenced as he is by empiricism — he never quite seems clearly to affirm that the intellect reaches genuine universals. Absent from Newman is St. Thomas's exaltation of human intelligence, at its highest, approaching the intuitive knowledge of the angels. The difference is more than anything a matter of epistemological method without prejudice to the orthodoxy of conclusions. While speaking quite different languages, the Angelic Doctor and Newman would have had no disagreements in any debate about the mutual dignity of faith and reason in the life of the soul: "I have no suspicion, and do not anticipate (any such suspicion) that I shall be found in substance to disagree with St. Thomas."[54] Breathing an air more redolent of Cappodocia than of Aquino, and in the context of a culture beleaguered by false intellectual economies, Newman wanted much to tell the same tale of the

---

[51]*Grammar*, p. 19.
[52]Ibid., p. 42.
[53]Ibid., p. 79.
[54]10 December, 1878, in *LD*, XXVIII, p. 421.

mind before God that the Scholastics had held to be true. He
had been somewhat scandalized, in fact, to find so little Thomism
when he first arrived in Rome as a Catholic; and his revival of the
early Fathers in support of reason as the servant of Christ was his
complementary version of what Leo XIII's *Aeterni Patris* would
undertake in enlisting a revival of the Scholastics. Not century
nor climate nor diction could divorce true doctors from this
principle of the mind at work on doctrine: "...the intellect
which is made for truth, can attain truth, and, having attained it
can keep it, can recognize it, and preserve the recognition."[55]

In earlier drafts, Newman had used "imaginative" for
"notional," and the change apparently was to make the assent
sound more kinetic, though neither Coleridge nor Newman ever
imputed any passivity to the imagination:

> According as the apprehension is notional or imaginative, so
> may the assent be called one or the other, the notional
> assent being languid, and the imaginative energetic. At the
> same time, though there are two kinds of apprehension (an
> intellectual apprehension of the meaning of a proposition,
> and the existential apprehension of the object of the
> proposition), there are not two kinds of assent: but in both
> cases it is one and the same assent in its nature given to
> different subject matters, in one case to notions, in the other
> to imaginations."[56]

But it is imagination nonetheless which confers reality, not by
knowledge or sight which appeal to the reason and sense, but by
belief as appeal to the imagination. And belief is the response to
probability. "Ten thousand difficulties do not make one doubt,"

---

[55] *Grammar*, p. 181.

[56] Preliminary ms. for *Grammar*, Ch. III, para. 1, 26-28 April 1868.
Vid. *RI*, p. 83. Cf. Newman to Wilfred Ward: "You seem to me to
insist, with an earnestness for which I doubt not you have some good
reason, on the difference between believing and realizing (which is
pretty much, I suppose, what in the 'Grammar of Assent' I have called
'Notional' and 'Real' assent)...," in Wilfrid Ward, *The Life of John
Henry Cardinal Newman* (London: 1912), Vol. II, p. 489.

the *Apologia* attests. Probability, then, denotes reliability rather than uncertainty.

As an example of the realization of assent as such, there is the figure of a schoolboy who has read Homer and Horace as an exercise, and they "at length come home to him, when long years have passed, and he has had experience of life, and pierce him, as if he had never before known them, with their sad earnestness and vivid exactness."[57] The image complements the telescoped one of C. S. Lewis whose schoolboy struggles with Greek poetry: "Of course, he gets it gradually; enjoyment creeps in upon the mere drudgery, and nobody could point to a day or an hour when he becomes able to desire it for its own sake; indeed, the power of so desiring it is itself a preliminary reward."[58]

"Simple assent" is an unconscious act of unconditional acceptance.[59] In religious terms it is material certitude, though technically it is neither certitude nor doubt. And as a characteristic it is commonly Protestant, even when a majority of Catholics also are familiar with it. "Complex assent," or reflex assent, is a conscious and deliberate act of unconditional acceptance. "Certitude" (as a mental state) is complex assent to a notional proposition; it is distinguished from certitude as a quality of propositions, being not a passive impression but an "active recognition of propositions as true, such as it is the duty of each individual himself to exercise at the bidding of reason, and when reason forbids, to withhold."[60] "Inference" is the conditional acceptance of a proposition; it is ratiocination, whose scientific form is logic and which is verbal reasoning.[61] "Formal inference" is logical acceptance; "Informal inference" is conditional acceptance based on accumulation of probabilities.[62]

---

[57]*Grammar*, p. 78. Cf. ibid., p. 10.
[58]C. S. Lewis, *The Weight of Glory* (Grand Rapids, Mich.: 1965), p. 3.
[59]*Grammar*, p. 159.
[60]Ibid., p. 345.
[61]Ibid., p. 263.
[62]Ibid., p. 288.

"Natural inference" is acceptance based on experience and practice.[63]

Now assent does not have the reasoning character possessed by inference: ". . . all men have reason, but not all men can give a reason."[64] But they are compatible: "Acts of inference are both the antecedents of assent before assenting, and its usual concomitants after assenting."[65]   The all-important "illative sense" is right judgment in ratiocination; that is, ratiocination as a perfection or virtue.[66] "Notional apprehension" pertains to inference; although it unconditionally accepts a proposition, inference accepts on the condition of the acceptance of a notion's premises. Real apprehension pertains to assent.

In addition, there are three ways of enunciating propositions: by doubt (expressed in a question), by inference (expressed in a conclusion), and assent (expressed in an assertion).   And of assertions there are five categories: profession, credence, opinion, presumption, and speculation.[67] Assertions, however, do not require assents. Assents, which are mental and not verbal, include some apprehension of the matter which is asserted. A mystery is a proposition, and a proposition can be assented to, provided it can be apprehended; and apprehension is implicit, since we would not know it to be a mystery had we not apprehended it. In effect, if we can discern that words express a mystery, we are capable of assenting to it. "Words which make nonsense, do not make a mystery."[68]

Then must follow a question, which is really the central question for conceptual reasoning in religion, namely: Can processes of inference end in a mystery? (Mystery here is meant as a thing inconceivable, since it is the co-existence of what seem

---

[63]Ibid., p. 330.
[64]*US*, p. 182.
[65]*Grammar*, p. 189.
[66]Ibid., p. 343; cf. pp. 361-362.
[67]Ibid., pp. 42ff.
[68]Ibid., p. 46; cf. p. 75.

to be incompatibilities; it is not merely incomprehensible, as are difficulties in the physical order). To the question, as Kant would answer no, Newman submits a solemn yes. His reply is based on the distinction between the notion of a thing and a thing itself, which, if a mystery, will have to be beyond adequate schematic representation by notion. By inference, the notion results in conclusion consistent with itself, though not consistent with the mystery to which it is inadequate.[69] Significantly, Newman illustrates with the example of metaphors, quite as though he were building his case on that of Coleridge for metaphor as the primary mode of certitude.

In the development of this time lies much of Newman's originality over against naturalism. And in the mysteries of revelation, as they are works of grace, Newman again parts with the naturalist in imputing to grace a power of action beyond simple moral influence: "... assent is ever assent; but in the assent which follows on divine announcement, and is vivified by a divine grace, there is, from the nature of the case, a transcendent adhesion of mind, intellectual and moral, and a special self-protection ..."[70] The empiricist epistemology is upheld ("Everyone who reasons is his own center"), but in matters supernatural in character, reason is aided by grace. And it is in the psychological response to grace that we have evidence of the personalism which Newman develops in order to rescue empiricism from nominalist individualism and its maddening solipsistic climate. For when all is said and done, the subtle distinction between assent and certitude requires not only that mind speak to mind in matters notional (the method of theology as a general system), but, as his cardinalatial motto would later aver, that the heart speaks to heart in matters real (the method of religion as having to do with particulars). "The heart is commonly reached not through the reason but through the

---

[69]Ibid., p. 47.
[70]Ibid., pp. 186-187.

imagination, by means of direct impressions, by testimony of facts and events, by history, by description . . ." etc., as we noted at the beginning of this essay.[71]

Appeals to reason are not only not discredited, then, they actually find their proper resolution in real assent. Dogmatic statements are not apprehended well if the intellect receives from them only "the subtlety, the aridity, the coldness of mere scholastic science." Addressed to the imagination as much as to the pure intellect (or, as Kant would have it, to the reason alone), they give birth to noble hymns.[72] If Locke and Hume lend their voices to the account of notional assent, Coleridge and Wordsworth are heard here. As a practiced fact more than a theory, this was nothing newer than the venerable incantatory tradition from Aquinas and Bernard through John of Damascus and Ephraem Syrus to the Apostle himself.

In the Coleridgean account of it, poetical lyricism is evidence of the reason at work precisely when it is an ode born of the imagination perception. Reason moves the mind to give the imagination full initiative in religious experience. Yet Coleridge's own verse, objectively superior in diction to Newman's, had about it a neurotic impressionism where Newman was classically emotive. As a poem which the author thought would give the most pleasure by being imperfectly understood, "Kubla Khan" begins a rumble which would become the howl of modern free verse mated to chaotic thought. It is the doxology of a religion without revelation, a sign that religiosity, and not religion, is the opiate of the masses. Newman appraised the type whose religion is an "inchoation" which "needs a complement": "A religious man who has not the blessing of the infallible teaching of revelation is led to look for it for the very reason that he is religious. He has something but not all; and if he did not desire more it would be proof that he had not used, that he had

---

[71]Ibid., p. 139.
[72]Ibid.

not profited by what he had. Hence, he will be on the look-out. Such is the definition, I may say, of every religious man who has not the knowledge of Christ: he is on the look-out."[73]

The Laudian divines had provided seventeenth century roots for much of the Victorian definition of doctrine; but, much as Newman revered them all his life, he required a system of his own to explain how the substance of belief should be believable to minds wounded by the depredations of naturalism. The neo-Idealism of Coleridge had failed to do it, only erecting a sectarian romanticism of "the universal, the eternal and the necessary" administered for human convenience by clerks of harmless erudition.[74] And though Newman may sound at times like the proposer of little more than an extension of Butler, he addressed a culture which had come to take for granted the scientific biology and romanticism which were blank pages to Butler. Newman's empiricism disposed him to the scientific outlook, and his own psychology and theory of imagination made him the most mature of romantics. It was as though he wanted to shine an eighteenth century light through a Victorian painted glass without smashing the window as the Liberals were doing in their metaphysical clumsiness. If he was not exactly a living specter like Dr. Routh who wore his powdered wig at Magdalen College well into the nineteenth century, he does retain the powerful clarity of an earlier empiricism. And with it he does two things. First, he conflates the Gospel account of creation with what materialists, in their legitimate realm, perceived of creation psychologically. But second, he rattles the tendency of the materialists to describe knowledge exclusively by a sensate interior psychology. Like some modest Colossus almost shy about his pose, he straddles the ages of reason and romance and preaches to both:

---

[73]Ibid., p. 417; cf. p. 486.
[74]Cf. Fausset, op. cit., p. 321.

> As Faith may be viewed as opposed to Reason, in the
> popular sense of the latter word, it must not be overlooked
> that Unbelief is opposed to Reason also. Unbelief, indeed,
> considers itself especially rational, or critical of evidence;
> but it criticizes the evidence of Religion, only because it
> does not like it, and really goes upon presumptions and
> prejudices as much as faith does, only presumptions of an
> opposite nature.[75]

Reluctant to discount the capacity of reason to assimilate
revealed truths, he limits the rational response to the self-
authenticating impression of revelation only to the degree that
analysis and description are inadequate accounts of the initial
impression made by the object of revelation. Religious speech,
then, is bound to be more suggestive and apophatic than
descriptive, though it is not irrational for that. There is even a
hint of this in Newman's treatment of infallibility which, in the
particular instance of papal infallibility, is a negative diction for
what is not true at least as much as it is a specific formulation of
what is true; and here he anticipates and faults a very modern
instance, that of the theologian who would assume that any item
in ordinary magisterial discourse does not require obedience
since it is not positively specified as infallible.[76] As he had said in
the history of the Arians, "freedom from symbols and articles is
abstractedly the highest state of Christian communion, and the
peculiar privilege of the primitive church."[77]

His "inopportunist" position on the definition of papal
infallibility, which dogma he full supported, only questioned the
timing of the definition. It is an example of his sensitivity to the
respective claims of notional and real assents: papal infallibility
appeals notionally, and it is left to the conscience acting within
historical circumstances to assent really. The universal

---

[75]*US*, pp. 233-234.

[76]Cf. *LD*, XXV, p. 329.

[77]John Henry Newman, *The Arians of the Fourth Century*
(Westminster, Md.: 1968, orig. 1833), p. 36. Cf. "NET," p. 82.

interpretation of this has been expressed in contemporary idiom by Pope John Paul II for whom the synthesis between faith and culture is no less important for faith than it is for culture, and "a faith which does not become culture is a faith which has not been fully received . . ."[78] Newman writes in a letter shortly after the appearance of the *Grammar*: "No abstract definition can determine particular fact." He would not deny the truth of the Vatican Council formulation in any way, and his private spiritual devotions make frequent reference to papal claim upon obedience, but he would explain its implications for assent: ". . . hitherto (the Pope) has done what he would, because its limits (i.e. of his power) were not defined — now he must act by rule."[79]

A New Case for Certitude

In deference to its empiricist roots, the first concern of the *Grammar* is not the object of faith but the method of its apprehension. Newman proposes to refute the subjectivism of Hume and other sceptical antecedents this way: the object of faith is of a scale so vast that human utterance is unable to declare it precisely, thus the content of revelation remains distant from thought of it and language descriptive of it. While Kant was willing to stand stoically unconsoled in the face of this inaccessibility, Newman took the opposite and braver tack, hardly out of a psycho-pathological need for the consolations of certitude but rather drawn as a magnet to a palpable absence in contemporary consciousness, a void carved by an "aboriginal calamity" which had separated men from the God who nonetheless truly exists.

---

[78]Pope John Paul II to the Sixth Symposium of the Council of European Episcopal Conferences, 1982.

[79]*LD*, XXV, p. 309.

Kant and Newman provide the two strains, secular and religious, which form the fugue of nineteenth century romanticism and a prelude to philosophical unwindings of the twentieth century.   Newman described tension in his own experience: "If I looked into a mirror, and did not see my face, I should have the sort of feeling which actually comes upon me, when I look into this living busy world, and see no reflection of its Creator ... Were it not for this voice, speaking in my conscience and my heart, I should be an atheist, or a pantheist, or a polytheist when I looked into the world."[80]

The resolution is a modified Coleridgean picture of belief commanding certitude when it is credible primarily to the imagination.   In its fundamental import, this means that the Christian is compelled by the image of Christ more than by opinions about him.   God is a self-sufficient whole, and so he gives a unified impression of himself, and not a system to explain himself, though a system can later be induced.   By "seeing" this Object, the imagination motivates or energizes real assent.   Still, this real assent does not ensure the truth of what is assented to. A "true believer" in the popular derogatory sense of the term, can be a wrong believer.   And thus Newman confounds Idealism: "It seems to me unphilosophical to speak of trusting ourselves. We are what we are, and we use, not trust, our faculties ... We act according to our nature, by means of ourselves, when we remember or reason.   We are as little able to accept or reject our mental constitution, as our being.   We have not the option; we can but misuse or mar its functions.   We do not confront or bargain with ourselves; and therefore I cannot call the trustworthiness of the faculties of memory and reasoning one of our first principles."[81]

But whence, then, comes verification?   Butler's argument from accumulated probabilities is offered in the section on

---

[80]*Apologia*, p. 217.
[81]*Grammar*, p. 61.

informal inference; negatively, it is an argument for the improbability of unbelief and drifts close to Pascal's *il faut parier*: "Probable proofs being added not only increase the evidence but multiply it ... The truth of our religion, like the truth of common matters, is to be judged by all the evidence taken together. And unless the whole series of things which matter be alleged to have been by accident (for here the stress of the argument for Christianity lies) then is the truth proved."[82]   And if the probability argument is not what traditionally characterized the affirmation of faith, Newman's justification is a diffident, if not resigned, dismissal: "Such an accusation does not give me much concern. Everyone who thinks on these subjects takes a course of his own."[83]

He has in fact recognized Butler's limitations "understood or misunderstood to teach" in that Liberal Protestants have taken the structure of probabilities assented to as their highest opinion in religion, when opinion is taken to mean notional assent.[84] Such, of course, runs the danger of multiple opinions. This is acceptable insofar as these opinions are distinguished from dogmas. But as substitutes for dogmas they lead to the situation Newman would describe in his "Biglietto" address on the occasion of his becoming a Cardinal, when religion is a private mental luxury but not a public social truth. The spirit of Liberalism holds that all religious beliefs are to be tolerated for they are nothing more than matters of opinion, anyway.

So Newman moves to investigate the imagination in order to eliminate such Liberal superficiality. This is not inquiry, which is incompatible with assent because it suggests doubt. Investigation is the necessary method of development in doctrine. It discerns faith apart from prejudice by following the structure of sacred tradition. The final result is "a system or creed in the Reason"

---

[82]Joseph Butler, *Analogy of Religion* (London: 1836), pp. 329-330, in *Grammar*, p. 319.

[83]*Grammar*, p. 404.

[84]Ibid., p. 59.

formed from what had been "an impression on the
Imagination."[85] This system or creed, as an ecclesiastical fact,
sustains the primitive charisms of the Church when they were
free of "symbols and articles"; for while such was a privilege of
primitivism, it was a privilege peculiar to the Church when she
was close to the efficient events of her cause. And the ensuing
development of what Coleridge would call the "Enclesia," or
sacred linguistic community, now provides a clear statement of
what belief can say about itself in its older age.

If after all this, the concept of belief still seems suspiciously
unscientific, Newman can hardly be at fault. Or if he should
seem to be so, then he obliquely comes to his own defense:
". . . in a philosopher it is even a merit to be not altogether vague,
inchoate and obscure in his teaching; and if he fails even of this
low standard of language, we remind ourselves that his obscurity
perhaps is owing to his depth."[86] Belief is a thing clear in itself
only at the end of a development from notional assent and
inference: "First comes knowledge, then a view, then reasoning,
then belief."[87]

To remain only in notions is to be stamped as that
"gentleman" who is so ironically the object of examination in the
Idea of a University, whose knowledge is not useless, "but it is
never more than the furniture of the mind . . . it is never
thoroughly assimilated with it."[88] Such assimilation is the
property of the whole man. And because the belief or credibility
which makes probability certain is exacted from the whole
personality, it is not rational, as notional assent would be, but
imaginative. In a psychological way of speaking, belief as real
assent is a creative act which helps to accomplish personal
identity. The history of the Church and her saints is the
representative evidence of this and, thus, the anchor and point of

---

[85]Development, p. 49.
[86]Grammar, p. 21.
[87]Ibid., p. 92.
[88]Ibid., p. 55.

reference for all probability. The "Biglietto" address is the *summa* of the fact: the particular mode by which Providence rescues the Church is uncertain, but all history bears witness to the fact that Providence has never failed.

As the sources of Newman's criticism have interested many, the results have interested more. And among them are those who have detected in it a Modernist tinge, as though from one angle Newman was as destructive of objectivity as Kant was from another. It is true that Newman upset ultramontanists by moving beyond the univocal language of the Scholastics. They feared that once a distinction is made between the content of revelation and the language used to describe it, there may appear to be a wide and even (for the Modernist) an insuperable chasm between the metaphors of faith and the formulas of belief. But while poets early as Arnold saw it just that way, Coleridge and Newman thought that metaphor actually became a reliable bridge between faith and its object.

The magnanimous patience of Newman would have had no toleration for the contemporary laziness which introduces various forms of fuzziness under the label "nuanced." He was for varieties of method, but this was not the pluralism taught by minds of lesser loyalty to the deposit of faith. The new Cardinal quoted the Liberal voice as asking what difference does it make if a man puts on a new religion every morning. For him, it made all the difference. The *Grammar* was written to refute such sentimentality masquerading as imagination. The danger of Newman's exposition, of course, must always be its susceptibility to abuse by those of less steady commitments. As regards his own integrity of belief, the unequivocal judgment of Pius X on Newman was offered to Bishop O'Dwyer of Limerick: "Indeed, though things might be found which appear different from the usual theological mode of expression, nothing can be found which would arouse any suspicion of his faith . . ."[89]

---

[89]*Acta Apostolicae Sedis* 1908, XLI, p. 200. Cf. *NMW*, p. 224, fn. 7.

The roots of Newman's theory are deep, but they are not tangled, not if the psychologisms of his beloved Cappodocians are not tangled. They probably influenced him even more than the empiricist critique of Butler and Coleridge's literary agency on behalf of the imagination. The only possible recapitulation of the *Grammar* in one line may be no ordinary line, but the line of his own memorial inscription: "Ex umbris et imaginibus in veritatem." A study of sources cannot trace all that those words portend, nor can it efface the originality of the man who chose them. But what Newman said is more important than who taught him to say it. Newman covered his own cause in the cause of another:

> It would have been absurd to prohibit the controversy which has lately been held concerning the obligations of Newton to Pascal; and supposing it had issued in their being established, the partisans of Newton would not have thought it necessary to renounce their certitude of the law of gravitation itself, on the ground that they had been mistaken in their certitude that Newton discovered it.[90]

---

[90]*Grammar*, p. 230.

Kähler on Historical
and Historic Truth

The Problem of Historicism

Albert Schweitzer made a remark whose preening is all the
more embarrassing from the lips of one who in the mid-twentieth
century was received as a saint without need of a Church:
"... nowhere save in the German temperament can there be
found in the same perfection the living complex of conditions and
factors — of philosophic thought, critical acumen, historical
insight, and religious feeling — without which no deep theology
is possible."[1] But a *Volk* with the best potential for deep theology
also has the best potential for deep theological error. Schweitzer
saw the finest example of German theological precision in the
critical investigation of the life of Jesus. He also acknowledged
that the splendid faculties brought to this work had not
accomplished the objectivity which was its singular purpose. It
created an extravagant form of subjectivism about God and
called it objective: "... each individual created Him in
accordance with his own character."[2]

Fourteen years before that estimation, Martin Kähler (1835-
1912), Professor of New Testament and Systematic Theology at
Halle, passed a more radical judgment on historical criticism:
purely historical research applied to the Bible was not scientific
because it was science applied outside its domain. It was a

---

[1]Albert Schweitzer, *The Quest of the Historical Jesus*, 3rd ed.,
(London: 1950, orig. 1910), p. 1.

[2]Ibid., p. 4.

scientism, history turned into ideology. And this in turn made history historicism, a false version of history which isolated certain facts from the Gospel and pieced them together into a neo-Gospel for reductionist tastes.

As a corrective, in 1896 Kähler published a series of addresses under the title "The So-Called Historical Jesus and Historic, Biblical Christ." Though he disagreed with Herrmann on many points, he agreed with him on this: faith is a final and total commitment, and as such it must be based on something more lasting than historical research which by its nature revises itself. Drawing on Luther, but consistent with the apostolic tradition right through its reiteration in the Roman Catechism after Trent, Kähler locates preaching as the *primum officium* of the Church in the economy of justification; and so the authentic Christ is to be found not in artifacts about him but in the preaching about him. Barth remarks the influence of Beck on this reaction against the Enlightenment historicists, and Kähler grants it himself:

> The great reality of the Bible has always prevented me from simply putting it in the same category as other literary productions. That is to say, I came to the same conclusion with respect to Holy Scripture as with respect to the person of Jesus. By the reality of the Bible I mean what the Bible has been in history and what it has come to mean for my life. Gratitude compels me to mention here the influence which Johann Tobias Beck has exercised upon me in this respect. I should also mention the way in which he taught me to approach the Bible and to hold to it without detailed theories about its nature and origin. What the Bible has meant in history and in my life are two facts which confirm each other. Had I not caught sight of the first and had I not been so powerfully overwhelmed by it, I would not have been spared the temptation to explain away my own experience psychologically and to divest it of its spiritual meaning.[3]

---

[3]Martin Kähler, *The So-Called Historical Jesus and the Historic, Biblical Christ*, trans. Carl E. Braaten (Philadelphia: 1964), p. 122. Cf.

As the "Father of Form Criticism," while not technically a form critic in his own method or design, Kähler also had an indirect precursor in Wilhelm Martin Leberecht De Wette (1780-1849), a professor at Heidelberg, at Berlin where he was a colleague of Schleiermacher, and at Basel. This underestimated figure was probably the first to discern the discourses of Jesus from the apostolic teaching, tracing various traditions within the latter. By respecting the texts as testimonies rather than as formal biographies, this would evolve into form criticism, isolating texts according to their proper *genres*. But what particularly sets a pattern for Kähler's exegesis is a principle to which De Wette gives a unique place: "All that in terms of content and form belongs to science and practice we omit and take into consideration as the heart of the matter only what belongs to faith."[4]

Assertion of the priority of faith was aimed at the absurdity of the Ritschlian thesis. Kähler denied any reduced separation of Jewish and Gentile Christianities. This did not capture much attention at first, and indeed was largely ignored while Kähler lived. The second edition of Kähler's work in 1896 was not reprinted until 1928, and the original edition reappeared in 1953. Only since then has Kähler been given his due.[5] But inasmuch as Ritschl and Kähler, totally distinct in critical method, centered on a doctrine of reconciliation to define the core of faith, they jointly form a pedestal for Barth, a support for Barth's early grasp of *Romans*, for instance. But the focus is also a reason for

---

Karl Barth, *Protestant Theology in the Nineteenth Century* (London: 1972), p. 622.

[4]*Textbook of Christian Dogmatics Presented in its Historical Development* (Berlin: 1813), pp. 19-20, in Werner Georg Kümmel, *The New Testament — The History of the Investigation and Problems* (London: 1973), p. 106.

[5]Vid. James A. Robinson, *A New Quest of the Historical Jesus* (Philadelphia: 1983), p. 31. The second edition of Kähler's work in 1896 was reprinted in 1928 and the original edition was reissued in 1953.

the eclipse of all three now when justification no longer determines the agenda for dogmatic theology.

Even Kähler at least hinted that Luther's atonement faith was more derivative from the Church's penitential life than from the New Testament evidences. Resurrection eschatology is now more generally recognized as the cause for the Gospel being the Gospel. But this owes much to Kähler's juxtaposition of the historical Jesus and the historic Christ. The distinction was his attempt to counter the subjectivism of three particular voices: Schleiermacher who had reduced the objectivity of revelation to religious "feeling"; von Hofmann who had refashioned the facts of redemption chiefly as the items of faith experienced *a priori* by the convinced Christian and only secondarily as the evidence of Scripture; and Herrmann's counterproductive appeal to defeat subjectivism by separating the basis of faith (the historical Jesus) from the content of faith (the biblical Christ).

Kähler's course was both subtle and unambiguous. The basis of faith and the content of faith are perceived in different ways but are interdependent. We believe a thing that happened, but we believe it not just because it happened but because we know it to have happened. We cannot know a Christ who is not historical (*historische*), but we know him as Christ because he is historic (*geschichtliche*), or supra-historical. The terms are obscure in English, but the distinction is crucial lest one think Kähler disregards the importance of historical fact. The historical Jesus is not termed "so-called" because he did not exist, but because his existence is not a suitable object for historical-critical research. The historic Christ is the content of preaching and cannot be judged worthy of being that by a false aura of scientific detachment.

Although Tillich did not think Kähler was a guide for questions raised later in the demythologization controversies, he used his categories when he called the "historical Jesus" irrelevant. As Braaten reminds critics, Tillich was not relying primarily on an Hegelian dialectic of the "Jesus of history" and the "idea of Christ."[6] Tillich drew proximately on Kähler's system of *historische Jesus* and *geschichtliche Christus*. As we shall see, the "idea" theory which has so haunted and damaged modern analysis, was suspected and even scorned by Kähler. It eventually became the ground for his abuse of the historicists, even though his own freedom from it was problematic at best.

Kähler the Critic

> Today everyone is on his guard when a dogma is presented frankly as such. But when Christology appears in the form of a "Life of Jesus," there are not many who will perceive the stage manager behind the scenes, manipulating, according to his own dogmatic script, the fascinating spectacle of a colorful biography. Yet no one can detect the hidden dogmatician so well as a person who is himself a dogmatician, whose job it is to pursue consciously and intentionally the implications of basic ideas in all their specific nuances. Therefore, the dogmatician has the right to set up a warning sign before the allegedly presuppositionless historical research that ceases to do real research and turns instead to a fanciful reshaping of data.[7]

Schweitzer agreed, but was no less certain, that beneath the layered restorations worked by clumsy historical investigators would be found a portrait of the Jesus who transcends history. Schweitzer has been faulted for failing to credit Kähler's work; the detailed index to *The Quest of the Historical Jesus* has not a single citation of the man from Halle. Robinson says this is only because Kähler did not come into prominence until the rise of form criticism after the First World War.[8] But that must be because lights like Schweitzer ignored him. Kähler was hardly

---

[6]Carl E. Braaten, intro. to *The So-Called Historical Jesus*, op. cit., p. 20.

[7]*The So-Called Historical Jesus*, op. cit., pp. 56-57.

[8]Robinson, op. cit., p. 172.

unknown, and by the time of the *Quest*, Kähler's *So-Called Historical Jesus* was in its second edition. The omission is particularly odd in a work which is an historical survey of research "from Reimarus to Wrede." Barth's *Protestant Theology in the Nineteenth Century* gives Schweitzer and Kähler brief but equal treatment. It may be that Schweitzer distanced himself from the conservative reading which Kähler gave the kerygma of the Gospel books once he had discerned its form.

Kähler rejected any use of the New Testament to furnish historical data. He would say that this was the mistake of prodigies like Harnack, and of simple souls who never cracked another book. The Bible is the proclamation of the historic to a world familiar only with things historical. The historic Christ is the portrait of the Savior and Lord understood according to the impact he had on his disciples. This Christ is preached and painted. There is no historical biography that transcribes and photographs him; such would satisfy curiosity, but it would elicit no lasting moral response. It could not make divinity grander, it could only parade it as grandeur: "We must not think that we can solve the problem with a pantograph, reproducing the general outlines of our own nature but with larger dimensions."[9]

We are facing an author who was as much an existentialist as Kierkegaard, even as he eschews the uncontrolled subjectivism of Kierkegaard's famous question, "How can something of a historical nature be decisive for an eternal happiness?"[10] That question certainly sounds more like Tillich than Kähler. Something historical *can* be decisive, and has been so in Christ, Kähler insists. But he also insists that it is decisive by virtue of what is historic in the historical. Kierkegaard did not make the distinction, and walked off alone after an anonymous figure whose reality has been whispered into his ear; Kähler tells of a

---

[9]*The So-Called Historical Jesus*, op. cit., p. 53.
[10]Søren Kierkegaard, *Concluding Unscientific Postscript*, trans. D. F. Swenson (Princeton: 1944), p. 86. Cf. Braaten, op. cit., p. 10.

Christ whose existence in history was not confined to time and space:

> ...from a purely historical point of view the truly historic element in any great figure is the discernible personal influence which he exercises upon later generations. But what is the decisive influence that Jesus had upon posterity? According to the Bible and church history it consisted in nothing else but the faith of the disciples, their conviction that in Jesus they had found the conqueror of guilt, sin, temptation, and death. From this one influence all others emanate; it is the criterion by which all the others stand or fall. This conviction of the disciples is summed up in the single affirmation, "Christ is Lord."[11]

And this affirmation becomes its own method:

> The risen Lord is not the historical Jesus *behind* the Gospels, but the Christ of the apostolic preaching, of the *whole* New Testament. To designate this Lord as "Christ" (Messiah) is to confess his historical mission, or as we say today, his vocation, or as our forefathers said, meaning essentially the same thing, his "threefold office." That is to say, to confess him as Christ is to confess his unique, supra-historical significance for the whole of humanity.[12]

The Jesus of Harnack and Liberal Protestantism can have no such significance, though he may be said to survive in the authentic remnants of his teaching. But remnants only indicate the whole cloth, Kähler would insist, and Jesus went to the cross in a seamless robe, singular in an incomparable perfection. That whole historic cloth cannot be bought at the price of the intellect. No intelligence, not even a Liberal one, is equipped to barter the psychology of perfection. It is won by a gamble, and a gamble greater than the costless one which gained some soldier a few historical threads while losing the historic One who had worn

---

[11]*The So-Called Historical Jesus*, op. cit., pp. 63-64.
[12]Ibid., p. 65.

them. To own this perfection demands the gamble of one's own life in an act of faith.

In Kähler's estimation, Herrmann was right to define Christian faith as Christ's final overpowering of the soul by the picture of him painted in the Bible, though the power does not begin with that portrait nor is it completed by it. There is a vaster picture bearing a more vivid character beyond human manipulation. Herrmann provided a portrait like one by Raphael or Reni, far finer than the rationalistic image made of dots and numbers, and the romantic cartoon left by "disgusting tirades of Renan."[13] Herrmann's image was fair enough for showing that Christ had a true face scarred by men; but it simply was not adequate to the subject. Needed is more than a figure "painted against a golden background," but the figure does have to be distinguishable from the background.[14] As Kierkegaard blamed Thorwaldsen for not showing the wounds, so Kähler objected to any artist who does not show the crown. Kähler really wants something quite like an ikon, a supra-dimensional face whose face is also the curtain of heaven. Nothing like it had been produced by German criticism, not even by Schweitzer imagining Christ haunting the shore of the sea. And it may be that the energy, and disappointment, of Kähler's thesis lies in its unawareness that such an image already exists.

He did not set out to defame the integrity of historical studies. By reacting against the particular tendencies of the "Life of Jesus" writers, he may seem to exaggerate the lack of source value in the Gospel. But if it is true, as Althaus has held, that the apologetic of our time needs a renewed emphasis on the texts as testimonies and sources, then Kähler in his day was only trying to correct an imbalance by asserting the primacy of testimony in a hierarchy of exegesis.[15] The proper order naturally would call

---

[13]Ibid., p. 55 n. 17.

[14]Ibid., p. 78.

[15]Cf. Paul Althaus, *The So-Called Kerygma and the Historical Jesus*, trans. David Cairns (Edinburgh: 1959), p. 48.

attention to what criticism could and could not hope to attain by its own design. In 1863 he had defended the validity of historical criticism, recommending the methodology of Ruckert and Reuss. And the method must respect the source of the sources: "The biblical text is to speak to its hearers as though the author, able to employ our idiom, were speaking to us today."[16] The quest of the historical Jesus by itself is a blind alley in this attempt, for the reason already given, that Christ does not rise from the dead in order to move back behind the texts. He is to be found in the entire New Testament understood as a proclamation.

Did Kähler mean to move Christianity from the context of history to the misty province of faith alone? Then he would be as voluntarist as Ritschl and the Erlangen school he wrote against. And only a serious matter moved him to write against anything, since he was not by nature a polemicist. He insisted upon the facticity of the redemption drama, but precisely as lived drama to be preached dramatically. It was not a scheme of propositions requiring assent simply because it was schematic. Kähler knew as well as Newman that martyrs do not die for conclusions. *Christus praedicatus* is the Christ of history, though also God of more than history. But the more is not less; the history he transcends is the history in which he appeared and against which he once was pinned.

One is baffled when Alistair McGrath says Kähler writes not as a New Testament scholar but as a systematic theologian. He was both, and a professor of both, and his "qualitative dialectic," to borrow from Kierkegaard, consisted in ascertaining their priorities. If he subordinated biblical criticism, only a biblicist could think that indicates an unqualified bias.[17] Nor is it clear why Mackey should be uncertain whether Kähler "takes the resurrection to be an event which made possible the faith of the disciples of Jesus and, indirectly, our faith also, or whether the

---

[16]Kähler, *Theologe und Christ*, in Kümmel, op. cit., p. 222.

[17]Vid. Alistair McGrath, "Justification and the Proclaimed Christ" in *Modern Theology*, Vol. I, No. 1 (Oct. 1984), p. 46.

preaching of the resurrection of Jesus is just another way of expressing the faith in him . . ."[18] Did not Kähler fault Herrmann for divorcing the historical Jesus from the biblical Christ? He was persuaded that the hidden Christology in the "lives of Jesus" was Arian or Ebionitic, and that modern historical research is weakened by a problematic prejudice against the resurrection. Discipleship responds to an historical event:

> The most effective of all the servants of the Nazarene, though not an eyewitness from the beginning, was nevertheless a witness of the risen Lord. Confidently he emphasizes that he had not received his gospel from men, even while drawing freely on the tradition concerning Jesus' life and teachings. This is more readily understood when we observe how little the witnesses troubled themselves about external matters, and yet how certain they were about the main things, namely, those of "dogmatic significance."[19]

Kähler, of course, was not the first to speak both of existential and factual history. Kierkegaard's rejection of Hegelian idealism had done that. But to the benefit of future dialectical theologians, Kähler respected the relevance of Christ to history as Kierkegaard had not. He traces the reductionist biographical obsession of the historicists to the abandonment of the Jesus of dogma for the "life-like and graphic Son of Man" with whom "the omniscient speculation of Hegel supplanted the dogmatics of Protestant Orthodoxy . . ."[20] Although he makes no reference to Kierkegaard, at times he can copy the resonance and the very language: "But when (Christ) steps among them declaring who he is, who is there who would not collapse in fear and trembling?"[21] In addition, he received from his teacher, Richard Rothem, the anti-Enlightenment disposition of Kant and

---

[18]James P. Mackey, *Jesus — The Man and the Myth* (London: 1979), p. 44.
[19]*The So-Called Historical Jesus*, op. cit., p. 89.
[20]Ibid., p. 44.
[21]Ibid., p. 45.

Schleiermacher. From this admixture he proceeded to channel a third and quite unexpected stream of theology flowing from Kantianism, the others being idealistic speculative thought and romantic neo-traditionalism.

So while much in the eclectic terminology of Kähler would seem to enlist the sympathies of Catholic Modernism, the difference lies in Kähler's attitude toward Idealism. Loisy, and derivatively Tyrrell, attacked the rational essentialists for not being sufficiently historical; Harnack's offense to them was not that he denied the supernatural Christ but that he denied Christ idealized. But his Christ is not intentially idealized as was theirs; he is supra-historical, a concept ultimately as befuddling to the immanentism of the Modernists as it was to Kant himself:

> The "unambiguous," idealized characters of drama are justly criticized as unrealistic figures. The biblical picture of Christ, so lifelike and unique beyond imagination, is not a poetic idealization originating in the human mind. The reality of Christ himself has left its ineffaceable impress upon this picture. Were this not so, all the scholars would long ago have ceased to rack their brains over the sphinx-like enigma of this person.[22]

Kähler was adamant. "Historical" may be admitted as an adjective in theology but never as a noun. The existentialism is not unfriendly to Kierkegaard's inward appropriation. But given the fact that Kähler is matching wits with the rationalist questers, one might allow for his studied neglect of the historian's virtues. Had he been dealing with Kierkegaard, he surely would have complained that history was appallingly absent from the economy of *angst*. His colleague, Max Reischle, took a more measured stance. Historical criticism can indeed reach to sources, but only when it understands its own methods. In words more pointed to a Harnack than to a Kähler, Reischle warns:

---

[22]Ibid., p. 79.

One must be doubly careful in asserting borrowings. It is a regulating principle of all historical scholarship that it attempts in the first instance to understand the individual phenomena of history in light of their own processes of development and only then resorts to the hypothesis of an alien influence. Above all and as a further consideration, the theologian has a duty which is not merely an opportunistic calculation, but his vocation to serve the Christian community: namely, that of exercising special caution . . .[23]

Kähler was more conservative in this line than, for example, Schweitzer, who speaks of an "abiding and eternal Jesus" who is "absolutely independent of historical knowledge and can only be understood with His spirit which is still at work in the world."[24] Kähler recognizes more than a spirit at work, or such would be subjective indeed, a faith built on faith, were it not the spirit of Christ truly raised from the dead.

Liberal critics may complain that he makes this point by identifying the kerygmatic tradition of the Gospel too closely with St. Paul.[25] Kähler would brush the complaint aside as a suspect sign that the critics themselves lacked right faith in the preached Christ:

From these fragmentary traditions, these half-understood recollections, these portrayals colored by the writers' individual personalities, these heartfelt confessions, these sermons proclaiming him as Saviour, there gazes upon us a vivid and coherent image of a Man, an image we never fail to recognize.   Hence, we may conclude that in his unique and powerful personality and by his incomparable deeds and life (including his resurrection appearances) this man

---

[23]Max Reischle, "Biblische Theologie" in *Realencyklopadie fur Protestantische Theologie und Kirche*, 3rd ed., 1896-1913, Vol. III (1897), p. 197; cf. Kümmel, p. 317.

[24]Albert Schweitzer, *The Quest of the Historical Jesus*, (London: 1954), p. 399.

[25]Cf. eg., Howard Clark Kee, *Jesus in History* (New York: 1970), p. 111.

has engraved his image on the mind and memory of his followers with such sharp and deeply etched features that it could be neither obliterated nor distorted.[26]

How much more vivid and inescapable is this figure who declares himself, in comparison with Schweitzer's albeit more poetic Jesus whose anonymity would distract even Kierkegaard: "He comes to us as One unknown, without a name, as of old, by the lakeside, He came to those men who knew Him not."[27] What Mackey said of this, Kähler could have said: "The sentence has an inspiring sound, and makes no sense." And it cannot make sense without deference to the Church's declaration of what would otherwise indeed remain cloaked and unknown behind the texts:

> Is it not the case that this man (Schweitzer) who gives myth such an obvious place in his reproduction of the historical Jesus just as obviously mistakes the nature of the myth; for if the myth can only be understood as a literal and fanciful belief of (in this case) Jesus, then, of course, that poor deluded man could be at most the occasion, never the source, of what we have nevertheless managed to call the spirit of Jesus by means of some unexplained later refinement. And if the historical Jesus reached by history as Schweitzer reached him, can never function as our contact with the spirit of Jesus, what can so function or of what kind could this contact be? Some people will say something absolute and independent which they will be only too happy to call, mistakenly, faith. But Schweitzer does not know.[28]

Kähler does know and locates the intelligence in the fact of the Passion. And hence his key phrase, tucked in a footnote and confessed "provocatively," remarking how "one could call the Gospel passion narratives with extended introductions."[29]   It

---

[26]*The So-Called Historical Jesus*, op. cit., pp. 89-90.
[27]Schweitzer, op. cit., p. 401.
[28]Mackey, op. cit., p. 42.
[29]*The So-Called Historical Jesus*, op. cit., p. 80 n. 11.

clearly provoked many, and some witless critics responded by showing that Mark cannot be treated that way, as though Kähler did not know the Marcan structure; and that Kähler was mistaken to say that the Gospel books are "interested" not in *what* happened but in *who* acted and *how*, when he merely says that their purpose "is to report not so much *what* happened as *who* acted and *how*."[30]

History and Faith

A qualitative difference obtains between the assent of faith and the assent of history. The believer's judgment is absolutely convinced; the historian's judgment is qualified by the latest evidence.[31] As Kähler considers historical evidence inadequate for the judgment of faith, Bultmann appropriates Kähler's *historisch* and *geschichtlich* but in a manner which begs a docetic separation between objective history and faith. "Faith, being personal decision, cannot be dependent upon a historian's labours."[32] This is not the position Kähler takes when he says that the history of the New Testament and still less the history of the Jews had nothing to do with the summary confession of Christian faith: "Christ, the Lord." History is not irrelevant as it was to Bultmann who takes Kierkegaard to new lengths, saying flat out, "The Jesus of history is not kerygma, any more than my book was. For in the kerygma Jesus encounters us as the Christ — that is as the eschatological phenomenon *par excellence*."[33]

---

[30]Cf. eg., Kee, op. cit., p. 119.

[31]Cf. Van A. Harvey, *The Historian and the Believer* (London: 1969), p. 121.

[32]Rudolf Bultmann, *The Theology of the New Testament* (London: 1952), Vol. I, p. 26.

[33]Rudolf Bultmann, *Kerygma and Myth*, p. 117, in Robinson, op. cit., p. 31.

Biblical criticism is useful for Bultmann as it is not for Kähler, in that it is adequate to prove or disprove the historicity of events; but this historicity has no bearing on the meaning of Christianity which is found in the dynamic of the cross bringing man to a decision. Bultmann even alleges that the sayings of Christ are the invention of the early Church, but what shapes Christian life is the Church's affirmation about Jesus. Tillich (1886-1965) is more optimistic about the potential of biblical criticism than was Kähler who taught him. It is not a conduit for Christology, but it is a work of faith willing to examine itself. There is enough of the teacher in the student to prevent historicism from amounting to much, however: "Harnack was wrong... when he contrasted the message given by Jesus with the message about Jesus. There is no substantial difference between the message given by the Synoptic Jesus and the message about Jesus given in Paul's Epistles."[34]

An appreciation for paradox is needed if Harnack's subtleties are not to appear ambiguous. Is the authentic Christ historical as Bultmann might not allow, yet undisclosable by the texts as Tillich might not allow? Christ certainly is historical: "... so full of life, so real, it is as if we had seen him before our eyes. This is not the idealizing poetry of a human mind; his own essence has stamped itself here imperishably..."[35] Thus is refuted Herrmann's absolute equation of the historical Christ with the preached Christ, the fabrication of a fact from an idea. Kähler sees a circular sort of a task; after all, verification of the historical data makes faith dependent on critical research.[36] Scholarship of this kind can reach back to the faith of the early disciples. As it does so, it enriches faith, but it cannot vindicate the ground of that faith. The textual sources are too meager for adequate results and in no event can they apply to the psychology

---

[34]Paul Tillich, *Systematic Theology* (Chicago: 1957), Vol. II, pp. 117-118.
[35]*The So-Called Historical Jesus*, op. cit., p. 58.
[36]Ibid., pp. 144-147.

of development in Christ's teaching and his Messianic consciousness. Assumption of development must itself indicate a degree of historical conditioning, but no repristination of the texts can reach to the "real Jesus" as he was before the New Testament recorded impressions of his story. Trying to do that with either the rationalist knife or the idealist knife is like scratching the surface of a portrait to grasp the personality. "Tell the vision to no man ..." (Matt. 17:9) At best, we can come to learn something of the feel of the artist for the subject; at worst, and more often, we can only learn the mixture of the colors. "It is ... erroneous to make (faith) depend on uncertain statements about an allegedly reliable picture of Jesus which has been tortuously extracted by the modern method of historical research."[37]

There is a paradox, and a sublime one: confession of Jesus as the historic Christ is both indispensable and undemonstrable. The role of faith then takes its place at the heart of theological order, and Kähler gives *articulus iustifactionis* a determinative value greater than any Reformed theologian since Luther. The article of justification is not the doctrine of justification as such; it asserts the validity and immediacy of the power of Christ to reconcile man to God. Soteriology is applied Christology. Or, more precisely in Kähler's analysis, soteriology is applied *soterology*, i.e., the knowledge by faith, of Christ as Savior.[38]

> The real Christ, that is, the Christ who has exercised an influence in history, with whom millions have communed in childlike faith, and with whom the great witnesses of faith have been in communion — while striving, apprehending, triumphing, and proclaiming — *this real Christ is the Christ who is preached*. The Christ who is preached, however, is precisely the Christ of faith.[39]

---

[37]Ibid., pp. 72-73.
[38]Braaten, op. cit., p. 95 n. 31. Cf. McGrath, op. cit., p. 51.
[39]*The So-Called Historical Jesus*, op. cit., p. 66.

As a theological statement it is axiomatic and issues in theorems. But the axiom cannot be proved by known scientific methods. Historicism is a lame attempt to do just that, and must fail to do more than approach the statement. Kerygmatic preaching cannot be estimated by pseudo-science. Were such language part of his speech, Kähler might have said that the quest of the historical Jesus through the avenue of historicism is as futile as trying to observe transubstantiation through a microscope. The Scriptures are not the witness of a faith built only on faith, for they are more substantial than that; they are witness of faith to faith, and history is the record of the process, not its justification.

The Professor is certain of the witness of history, which is this: faith is not an isolated experience individualistic as well as individual. He insists as corrective of an assortment of thinkers, including Kierkegaard and Fichte, that the Christ who is preached is preached by the Church as the charismatic testimony of the whole company of the faithful. Individuals look in vain for raw data in the New Testament; that written record is itself the Church's interpretation of the data. "Underlying *credo in Christum* is a latent, but decisive *credo in ecclesiam.*"[40] As a result, the true Christ is discovered by an act of repentance which renders everyone an equal heir to the Church's proclamation. One will remember that Tyrrell found Fichte congenial because he dislocated this element from Christian life. Not so Kähler:

> In relation to Christ, whom we should trust and whom we dare to trust, the learned theologian must be no better off and no worse off than the simplest Christian: no better off, since he comes no closer to the living Saviour than anyone else; no worse off, since he too must overcome the obstacles to faith. To overcome these, there is only a single royal way: repent and believe the Good News, Jesus Christ died for our

---

[40]McGrath, op. cit., p. 49.

sins according to the Scriptures, and was buried and was raised on the third day according to the Scriptures.[41]

The believer should not be troubled by ambiguity of historical evidence. Rather, faith should be increased by it: "The more obscure the course of events remains which have preceded the literary activity, all the more certainly can we sense the invisible hand of Providence over the primitive community's carefreeness in the transmission of the tradition."[42]   Only forgeries are consistent. In testimony to the rule *lex orandi lex credendi*, there is no other way to certitude distinct from certainty, to employ again the grammar of Newman. While the circumstances of Christ's daily life can be submitted to historical analogy, the principle of analogy does not apply to his inner life which is different from ours in kind and not in degree. No science in the natural order finds a pattern for analogy to this, yet this in itself is far more positive than negative in its portent:

> Sinlessness is not merely a negative concept, the inner development of a sinless person is as inconceivable to us as life on the Sandwich Islands is to a Laplander. In the depths of our being we are different from him, so different in fact that we could become like him only through a new birth, a new creation. How then can we hope to analyze and explain Jesus' development, its stages and changes, in analogy with the common experience of humanity?   Indeed, if we look deeper we encounter the objection, How could he have been sinless in the midst of a world, a family, and a people full of offense? . . . All this is a miracle which cannot be explained merely in terms of an innocent disposition. It is conceivable only because this infant entered upon his earthly existence with a prior endowment quite different from our own, because in all the forms and stages of his inner life an absolutely independent will was expressing itself, because God's grace and truth became incarnate in him.[43]

---

[41]*The So-Called Historical Jesus*, op. cit., p. 73.
[42]Ibid., p. 90.
[43]Ibid., pp. 53-54.

A Papacy of Scholars

The vast difference between Christ and other humans is not a fabulous docetism. It is a difference neither hostile nor inaccessible to human reason. It will not be comprehended, however, by human initiatives toward him. The coming of Christ to man is what initiates justification. A grave fault of historical criticism has been the tendency to reduce this structure to a predetermined comprehensibility, fabricating an immediate notion of the Messianic character and its capacities. "... the necessary application of the principle of analogy in any such reconstruction excludes from the outset any supra-historical or transcendent understanding of the person of Christ, so that an Ebionite Christology results simply through the historiographical process itself."[44]

Any method which separates the historical Jesus from his proclamation confines itself to an *a priori* philosophical assumption of what is possible and impossible; hence Kähler's Pascalian censoriousness of critics who require "a head schooled in philosophy" to justify faith. There is no tone of romantic nostalgia in this, no defense of cognitive deviants; he could be quite as critical of Roman Catholic traditional Protestant systems which in his estimation tamed Christ on tight leashes.

> The Jesus of the "life-of-Jesus" movement is merely a modern example of human creativity, and not an iota better than the notorious dogmatic Christ of Byzantine Christology. One is as far removed from the real Christ as is the other. In this respect historicism is just as arbitrary, just as humanly arrogant, just as impertinent and "faithlessly gnostic" as that dogmatism which in its day was also considered modern.[45]

---

[44]Ibid., pp. 49-50.
[45]Ibid., p. 43.

Kähler could declare how useless is Christology "from below to above," as it separates the Jesus of history from the Jesus of an inescapable Passion and Resurrection. Historicism leads to a dead-end, or the blind alley he mentions in his opening sentence, when it follows the liturgical texts of early Christianity as though they were maps. It can hardly be denied that his warnings about faithless gnosticism have been realized in the instance of today's neo-historicists who dismiss as "culturally conditioned" any Gospel evidence which runs counter to the received ideological agenda for Church and society. He had already felt it in the air: "In most instances... modern biographers share the biblical point of view only to a very limited extent. In fact, not a few deliberately set themselves against 'the antiquated world view of the New Testament'..."[46]

Scripture study properly respects the two characteristics of Christ's lasting meaning: that he evoked faith from his disciples, and that the disciples confessed this faith. Such respect demands a mediation between past and present. It is the appropriate task, not of historical study, but of dogmatics which can discriminate between valid and invalid uses of historical criticism: "The task of dogmatics is to provide an inventory of our assets."[47]

Our friend then urges the dogmatician to enter the lists against the "papacy of learning" and the "pontificating of the historians." John Macquarrie attributes the language to Paul Althaus; but the source is Kähler, showing his attitude to papalism and historicism alike.[48] It is a Catholic tenet that the Pope has a right to be papal. But there are many little popes, there being no shortage of vocations to the papacy; and if they were the historicists of Kähler's world, they are no less conspicuous today. They may even be more blatantly known as, for example, among some liturgists who have taken upon

---

[46]Ibid., p. 56.
[47]Ibid., p. 66.
[48]Althaus, op. cit., p. 69. Cf. John Macquarrie, *The Scope of Demythologizing* (London: 1960), p. 246.

themselves the reformulation of dogma. But the point is the same: where there is no prejudice in favor of the preached Christ, the preached Christ will become a prejudice. Liturgical experts who "recover" the worship of the primitive Church in a version conformed to their bourgeois anthropology are guilty of the same theosophy by which Ernest Bosc claimed that the real Jesus was not a Semite but an Aryan. Much of the redesigning of dogma and worship in liberal Catholic circles has only updated the *Kulturkampf* of the nineteenth century. Schweitzer surely was more than tainted with it, but gave an opinion: "... modern theology ... mixes history with everything and ends by being proud of the skill with which it finds its own thoughts — even to its beggarly pseudo-metaphysic with which it has banished genuine speculative metaphysics from the sphere of religion — in Jesus and represents Him as expressing them."[49]

Kähler cannot escape the criticism which his "supra-historical" dichotomy between existence and facts provokes. Historicism is one thing, but literary and form criticism cannot be dismissed altogether as incompatible with the analysis of faith. He would have to come to terms today with the way historical criticism is being applied at least as much to amplify the primitive witness as to reduce it. Witness the recent remarks of Pope John Paul II on "prodigies and signs" as part of the essential testimony to Christ of the Gospel: "Analysis of both text and context speaks in favor of their 'historical' character, and attests that they are events that actually happened and were truly wrought by Christ. Whoever approaches them with intellectual honesty and scientific expertise cannot dismiss them as mere later inventions."[50]

---

[49]Schweitzer, op. cit., pp. 398-399. Cf. ibid., p. 327 and Ernest Bosc, *La Vie ésoterique de Jésus Christ et les origines orientales du christianisme* (Paris: 1902), pp. 445ff.

[50]John Paul II, Audience, 11 Nov. 1987, in *The Tablet*, 28 Nov. 1987, Vol. 241, No. 7689, p. 1306.

Kähler on historicity fails to speak so blatantly, because he is limited by an undeveloped ecclesiology and sense of the sacred tradition. This is clear in such uninformed allegations as his charge that the Council of Trent propagated a religion without a Bible.[51] It is but another *Kulturkampf* cliché, ignorant of Trent's theology of the "Two Tables" of Word and Sacrament, a theology rooted in sources as ancient as Augustine and to be explicated by Pius XII.[52] This was the context of Pope John Paul's confidence in treating literary forms, and its absence was a ground of Kähler's nervousness.

There are three views of the Bible incomplete in themselves: as an historical source, as a book of devotion or edification, and as a book of doctrinal propositions. On this Kähler is admirably clear.[53] The propositional use is characteristic of confessional Protestantism from which he would distance himself. Then he must look for some kind of system which might prevent any of these views from abusing the purpose of revelation: "... the written Word does not exist merely and primarily for isolated individuals but for the living totality of the church and its members."[54] But the vision goes no deeper than that. In his attempt at intuition of the Church, he commits the same faulty historicism which he ascribes to biblical criticism. The Church functions only as a support system for those already involved in the kerygma: "This totality, the church of Christ, cannot, however, adopt for itself the standpoint of those who are just becoming Christians... Therefore the church acts and witnesses as the totality of believers for whose faith the written Word has obtained authority as the Word of God."[55] For all its

---

[51]*The So-Called Historical Jesus*, op. cit., p. 131.
[52]Cf. St. Augustine, *On Christian Doctrine*, III, 18, 26: PL 34, pp. 75-76; Pius XII, Encycl. "Divino Afflante Spiritu"; Con. Vatican II, *Dogmatic Constitution on Divine Revelation* "Dei Verbum," n. 12.
[53]*The So-Called Historical Jesus*, op. cit., p. 129.
[54]Ibid., p. 135.
[55]Ibid.

charismatic obligations to the preached Christ, Kähler's ecclesiology is functionally as reductionist as the historicist's Christology.

The argument is not strengthened by assuming that the Catholic system of metaphysics and tradition compromised justification by faith, or by excluding natural theology from the prologomena of dogmatics.[56] More cogent, though compounding the ambivalence of his thesis, is his rejection of the propositional use of Scripture by orthodox Protestantism. That old approach had made revelation contingent upon the certifiable accuracy of the biblical texts. Since faith is the faith of limited human capacities, it cannot enjoy the indefective reading of history unaided. But by caricaturing the weaknesses of historical criticism and investing faith with a science not its own, Kähler creates an imbalance which does not resolve excess and, in fact, makes it more restless. For as Mackey says, "... there is no reason to suppose that Kähler's restriction of the source and nature of faith to an area beyond historical research is any more balanced" than a "restriction of religious faith to a Kantian-type moral reason and its postulates."[57]

If Kähler resented a fossilized Gospel, as though it were a recreated Williamsburg compared to a living culture, then his resentment is even valiant. But all his protestations, without some intelligence of rational analysis, do not prevent him from leaning dangerously over into a potentially incoherent subjectivism of his own. He meant to rescue history from scepticism through the perspective of supra-historicity, while Herrmann tried the same through a moral matrix; yet the one no less than the other seems to argue for the historicity of Jesus precisely from an idea, as Frederick Gogarten had complained. If historicity does not refer to history, is it hard to imagine what its basis can be other than an idea. Fichte had been an "idea-of-

---

[56]Ibid.
[57]Mackey, op. cit., p. 46.

Christ" man, as had been Kant in his equation of the Son of God
with the "ideal of humanity well pleasing to God."[58] Theirs was
an *a priori* prejudice little different as a bias from what Kähler
read in the historicists. What then was the yield? It does seem
that when all has been gathered and accounted, the difference
between Kähler and the "Life of Jesus" critics is an example of
Carlyle's "difference between Orthodoxy or My-doxy and
Heterodoxy or Thy-doxy."

Though Kähler's supra-historicity was not idealist in the
technical sense, and could even confuse idealists, the appeal of
its *a priori* Christology was the sort which enticed the Modernists
into their misfortunes. And it remains a problem wherever
modern theological personalism is influenced by existentialist
philosophy. Only that which is spiritual is thought to be valid,
and this then builds an equation between Christ and our own
spiritual intuitions. What remains is a self-projection: the Christ
who challenges history is reshaped into a Christ who is little other
than man confirming himself. Here are roots of what in our own
time has become a cult of self-affirmation, pride parading as
piety.

Kähler's mistake is in the exaggeration of the truth about
the real Christ being the preached Christ. Vibrant heresies are
launched on the path of heterodoxy by the inflation of a truth
rather than by casting lots for a lie. And orthodoxy is such by
being a balance: not a *via media* between truths, but an
equilibrium of truths neither distended nor neglected. Kähler
rightly objected to an historicist Christology "from below to
above" because it makes man the initial agent in justification. He
lost his own balance by grabbing at a Christology in an isolation
from above to below; he simply did not adequately allow for the
freedom of divine grace in the historical tradition. The merit of
what Kähler had to offer is that it pointed to the central dignity

---

[58]Vid. Immanuel Kant, *Religion Within the Limits of Reason Alone*,
trans. Green and Hudson (New York: 1960), pp. 54ff.

of the Christ who is preached. Its wisdom would have been more profound had he considered more closely the implications of the supra-historical Christ preached by a supra-historical Church.

Harnack on the Essence
of Christianity

To the Basics Scientifically

"Improve yourselves! For God is in the process of bringing into being a new religious society." The paraphrase of Matthew 3:2, which even Goethe found amusing, helped place Karl Friedrich Bahrdt (1741-1792) in the front ranks of Enlightenment new-thinkers.[1] Goethe did not laugh at the Lisbon earthquake as it shattered the religious assumptions of his youth, nor did he dismiss the effort to make moral sense of what otherwise seemed either capricious or impotent in the God of religion. So Goethe was at one with the moralizing tenor of Enlightenment revisionism which took itself seriously. It certainly lacked the mellow gift to appreciate Austin Farrer's response when asked what God is trying to tell us in earthquakes: God is indicating that the crust of the earth should obey his laws for the movement of earth.

The impassioned neologists of the Enlightenment, a large number of whose heirs became modern Liberal Protestants, answered the question another way, abandoning objective revelation altogether and discounting those revealed dogmas for which unaided analysis had no explanation. Demons, the Eucharist, Hell, atonement and supernatural grace found no quarter in the new scepticism. As parts of a systematic economy, Christology and soteriology soon were questioned and a dim eye

---

[1]Cf. Karl Barth, *Protestant Theology in the Nineteenth Century* (London: 1972), p. 168, hereafter *PTNC*.

saw little plausibility in the Trinity, the divine inspiration of Scripture, or the divinity of Christ.

Adolf Harnack (1851-1930) stands near the end of the neological movement known to us as Liberal Protestantism. It was more than an updated rationalism. His Liberal Protestant critique was imbued with a Pietistic respect for doctrines judged less systematically than ethically and psychologically, although the intellectual equipment it could bring to the task was formidable. The objectivity of any assertion would be its adequacy for the soul's moral formation: the Gospel has "only one aim — the finding of the living God, the finding of Him by every individual as *his* God . . ."[2]

From the start a tension situates itself, trying to pursue this moral focus for the interior life by means of historical criticism freed from psychological prejudices. If the intention sounds elevated, the conclusions of its ambiguous method are not necessarily so. As Alec Vidler remarked of the Coleridgean maxim, that affirmations are mostly right and denials mostly wrong: "right in what they affirm, i.e. if they are not merely being clever in argument but are trying to articulate what they have proved on their pulses or what makes them tick . . ."[3] The Protestant Liberals did not deny God, as did cut-and-dried rationalists, though their practical account of him alienated from the metaphysical order was like rendering butter: what remainder of divinity finally floated to the surface was an incoherent and manipulatable force.

Harnack's predecessor, Johann Semler (1725-1791), for instance, rejected soteriology in the most explicit terms only to lapse into a combination of Rosicrucianism and mystical chemistry. It was a fate not unlike that of Giordano Bruno in the

---

[2]Adolf Harnack, *What is Christianity?* (London: 1901), p. 191, hereafter *WIC*.

[3]Alec Vidler, *Twentieth Century Defenders of the Faith* (London: 1965), p. 120, hereafter *TCDF*. Cf. Samuel T. Coleridge, *Biographia Literaria* (London: 1847), p. 254.

sixteenth century, however much his publicizers shrank from admitting it. Once dogma is declared inaccessible to reason (and once Bruno seduces with his portrayal of truth as "the daughter of time") the neologist tends to be left with neither dogma nor reason; and there is no guarantee that the void left by supernatural grace will be filled with something only natural and not unnatural. The unnatural may be a structure of fabricated assumptions in the form of rationalism; or it may be the disordered understanding of causality which is in fact superstition (the contemporary revival of gnosticism and "New Age" sorcery is the latest example); or it may become a piety of distracting inconsequence, as it did in the less piquant instances of German academics like Ritschl and his disciple who is the object of our immediate attention.

Yet even when most limited, the Liberal earnestness raises some to a nobility of purpose. Goethe would not have mocked the profession of faith which Johann Gottlieb Töllner (1724-1774) made on his deathbed:

> I am convinced of the divine mission of Jesus and of the truth of his story, which cannot have been invented. I am convinced of the divinity of his teaching, in which I find three things above all: a fine morality that can make men good and blessed in connection with the redeeming death of Jesus; and finally the doctrine of immortality and a better life to come. I know the probability of all this, which is provided by reason, but the world of Jesus alone gives me certainty: I live, and so you shall live. Now I see what is truly essential in religion, quite apart from the subtleties which do nothing to quiet me.[4]

Here is the seminal form of a Liberalism which would soon become far sparser in what it affirmed and quite more inclusive in what it nuanced. But Töllner's three articles make up the creed of creedless Christianity as Liberal Protestantism would

---

[4]Cf. Karl Aner, *Die Theologie der Lessingszeit*, p. 172, in *PTNC*, p. 166.

want it for a religionless religion. Their simplicity and resolve are early stages of the reductionist movement; for as affirmations to sceptics they are reservations for Christians. Cynicism was not the efficient motive. The new spirit in fact exuded an optimistic confidence carpentered from a combination of rationalism and, if it is not precipitous to say, crypto-romanticism, notwithstanding its mockery of the imagination. We shall return to this, but at least we can sense here why the supposed pessimism of the doctrine of original sin was rejected as flatly as Kant rejected it when he decided that grace itself contradicts human autonomy. Parenthetically, this perhaps is why Karl Barth approved of Aner's comparison of neology with the romantic "storm and stress" spirit even though Liberal Protestantism portrayed itself as a reasonable alternative to romanticism.[5]

How Liberal attitudes so quickly conditioned the intellectual climate of generations is a subject for a whole cultural anthropology; but that it did so is monumentalized by Harnack who, if not the most original of its spokesmen, was certainly the most rhetorical and grand. He was, of course, an academic but also a public figure of immense prestige and amiability, in a lifetime spanning the zenith and decay of the Liberal enterprise. His seven-volume *History of Dogma* (1885-1888) presents the Ritschlian formula of simple moral brotherhood depicted as having developed through the vicissitudes of politics and personalities into the concrete structure later known as Christianity. Caustic in diction and sweep, it quite more matches Kant than Coleridge in its anti-clericalism and summary dismissal of the early Christian Hellenizers. In matters ecclesiastical, Coleridge had submitted to the established order at least out of pragmatism. But even Kant at his most satirical would not have felt a need to edify the intentions of the Apostles. Not so Harnack for whom the "revisionist ardour of the Reformation went back ... to the very

---

[5]*PTNC*, p. 655.

beginning of religions ... the Reformation even modified or entirely put aside forms which existed even in the apostolic age ..."[6] These forms included fasting, the hierarchical structure of bishops and deacons, and chiliasm, for example; thus Harnack helped move Liberal Protestantism into an open profession of its split with traditional Christianity itself, rather as the latest tendency of Catholic modernism has been to repudiate Trinitarian theology and fundamental Christian anthropology.

He regrets that Luther failed to make a "clean sweep" and retained a form of doctrinalism. At the same time, the energetic mind of Harnack perceives a penalty in Luther's diminished respect for good works; and somewhat inconsistently, in light of some other criticisms, he regrets the loss of a good kind of "monasticism" consisting in persons living exclusively for the ends of the community in salutary dedication.[7] All in all, he is capable of joining the majority vote on Mars Hill against Paul of Tarsus: "...the way in which (St. Paul) ordered his religious conceptions, as the outcome of his speculative ideas, unmistakably exercised an influence in a wrong direction."[8]

A complaint is lodged against a Christology which starts the path to redemption with the Incarnation instead of an exemplarist ethic. Taken for what it is, Harnack's is not a Christology at all. "The Gospel, as Jesus proclaimed it, has to do with the Father only and not with the Son."[9] While he denies that this is rationalism (the word, he recognizes, has a bad odor in his lecture hall), he makes the title "Christ" a convention, neither Pauline nor Chalcedonian. Paul was an obscurantist from whom sprang "the speculative idea that not only was God in Christ, but that Christ himself was possessed of a peculiar nature of a heavenly kind," and the Councils were institutional impositions

---

[6]*WIC*, pp. 283-284.
[7]Ibid., pp. 285-292.
[8]Ibid., p. 184.
[9]Ibid., p. 144.

on plain fact, and at the very most, the divinity of Christ can only be a figure of speech for the sum total of his moral virtues.[10]

Harnack's lines are from the sixteen lectures of which *What is Christianity?* is composed. We would not have them had they not been transcribed by one of the six hundred students who heard them in the University of Berlin during the Winter Term 1899-1900. Whatever his final Christian reward has been, the young master of shorthand has preserved powerful evidence of a dynamic, if at times bombastic, style. The product went through fourteen editions in Germany alone between 1900 and 1927. It is all the more impressive for having been extemporaneous; and if that is a compliment, it may also be an excuse for the fatiguing diatribe to which the handsome rhetoric succumbs in the last five lectures. These last are similar to Kant's polemicism at the end of *Religion Within the Limits of Reason Alone*, though they lack his ironic cadenzas. If Harnack played to the galleries, they were filled, after all, with youths from the several faculties who may have tempted him to uncommonly shaky heights.

The essence of Christianity is plain enough, put forth with commensurate clarity even if the Christ of it wanders from the page. The essence is the teaching of Jesus, and the teaching has three tenets:

> Firstly, the kingdom of God and its coming.
> Secondly, God the Father and the infinite value of the
>   human soul.
> Thirdly, the higher righteousness and the commandment of
>   love.[11]

What Harnack holds to be the three uses of Scripture would appear to parallel these three tenets as their hermeneutic, though he does not systematize their agreement as such: they describe Jesus's teaching (the Kingdom of God); they show how his life served his vocation (which was to disclose the Fatherhood

---

[10]Ibid., p. 184.
[11]Ibid., p. 51.

of God and the soul's corresponding value); and they indicate the impression he made on his disciples (which was to communicate higher righteousness and love).[12]

Christianity as "something simple and sublime" should then come into human grasp, he hopes, for it means only one thing, the essence of the three essentials: "Eternal life in the midst of time, by the strength and under the eyes of God."[13] The elemental, basic, Christian vision morally interprets realized eschatology, but Harnack would avoid the expression here because of its metaphysical connotations. He does not think it a handicap to consider these questions about essence from so long a remove from early Christian experience. In fact, modern observation has the advantage of perspective, like an artist standing back from the canvas. The "kernel" may be distinguished from the "husk" better in Berlin than in Jerusalem, and certainly better than in Antioch or Alexandria.

> ... either the Gospel is in all respects identical with its earliest form, in which case it came with its time and has departed with it; or else it contains something which, under differing historical forms, is of permanent validity. The latter is the true view. The history of the Church shows us in its very commencement that "primitive Christianity" had to disappear in order that "Christianity" might remain; and in the same way in later ages one metamorphosis followed upon another. From the beginning it was a question of getting rid of formulas, correcting expectations, altering ways of feeling, and this is a process to which there is no end. But by the very fact that our survey embraces the whole course as well as the inception we enhance our standard of what is essential and of real value.[14]

So equivocal a thesis must have objective evidence going for it, and Harnack claims it does. He employs a method of historical science which "excludes the view of the question taken by the

---

[12]Ibid., p. 31.
[13]Ibid., p. 8.
[14]Ibid., pp. 13-14.

geologist and the religious philosophers."[15] He is too rational to
reject historical experience as irrelevant in the idealist manner.
Indeed, to the mind of this most accomplished historical
chronicler, Christian history is all-important and the true Christ
must be the historical Christ, discerned scientifically, free from
bias. Loyal to the rational confidence of Leibniz, history for
Harnack is a reliable mechanism independent of psychological
distortion: "In history absolute judgments are impossible...
History can only show how things have been... judgments are
the creation only of feelings and will; they are a subjective evil."
But then he unnervingly adds precisely such a judgment: "This is
a truth which in these days — I say advisedly in these days — is
clear and incontestable."[16]

Historical analysis considers Christianity under six
categories.[17] The first group of four is pastoral: asceticism, social
questions, public order, civilization.   The next couplet is
doctrinal: Christology and creed. In each he defines his words to
critique them, but the defining is idiosyncratic, and the
overwrought treatment of asceticism becomes an obsession as he
refutes the entire Christian spiritual tradition. Such scientism is
a highly unscientific revisionism. Harnack ignores Christ's own
fasts, and considers asceticism only as a pathology, even though
he later admits that the asceticism of the first Christians was not
unhealthy or dualist.[18] Nor is he unencumbered by an apologetic
of his own when he portrays mendicancy and monastic poverty as
ways of being "sentimentally coquetted with misery and
distress."[19]   And objectivity little obtains when he distances
himself from the evangelical counsel of sacrificial detachment:
"We must remember that in the Gospel we are in the East, and in
circumstances which from an economical point of view are

---

[15]Ibid., p. 6.
[16]Ibid., p. 18.
[17]Ibid., pp. 78ff.
[18]Ibid., pp. 86, 168.
[19]Ibid., p. 95.

somewhat undeveloped."[20]   There are advantages to being a
scholar at the golden end of the nineteenth century when one has
no king but the Kaiser. And they are advantages of an almost
singular kind; indeed, "... the Germans mark a stage in the
history of the Universal Church. No similar statement can be
made of the Slavs."[21]   The honors which the Prussian court
heaped on Harnack were the largesse of a public weal perceptive
as a hawk to notice a theory which could justify its aloofness from
prophetic correction. The Liberal movement laid the ground for
a civil religion which affirms and ritualizes the sympathetic goals
of the culture.

   A steady presentation of the Christian social vision emerges
which, motives notwithstanding, manages to censure the
unguarded enthusiasms of nascent "social gospel" ideas.
Harnack proposes a mature verdict: Christ is not a mere social
reformer.   The Gospel is profoundly communal and
individualistic at once because of the infinite value it imputes to
each soul. "Its object is to transform the socialism which rests on
the basis of conflicting interests into the socialism which rests on
the consciousness of a spiritual unity. In this sense its social
message can never be outbid."[22]

   The dramatic conception of history occurs to him, and he
even speaks of the "dramatic eschatological apparatus" of John
the Baptist. Both drama and eschatology then vanish in the
bleach of ambiguity about the meaning of John's preaching, as
apocalypse and repentance become a single duty of obeying the
eternal call to what is right and holy. The most dramatic element,
the covenant between God and man fulfilled in the atonement,
becomes a more or less static panel against which the
eschatological prophecies are pinned.   The overwhelming
concern is for assurance. The Fatherhood of God is of no
ecclesiological significance; it is exclusively an "inner union with

---

[20]Ibid., p. 97.
[21]Ibid., pp. 282-283.
[22]Ibid., p. 100.

God's will and God's kingdom, and a joyous certainty of possession of eternal blessings and protection from evil."[23] Atonement then is not a factor in effecting this union; and Christ's summons to "rejoice rather because your names are written in heaven" is reduced to a reminder to be conscious of our safety in God.[24]

An Intolerance of the Incomprehensible

From his empiricist background, Newman had defined mystery as the inconceivable co-existence of what look like incompatibilities. But the incompatibilities are not nonsense. From the rationalist background of Harnack, however, they are indeed nonsensical. Newman, then, referred incompatibilities to the judgment of historical probabilities and imagination. Kant simply drops the subject. He recognizes, at least formally, that such incompatibilities are unlike antinomies, or contradictions, in the physical world (which Newman points out are inconceivable but not incomprehensible). Kant will not consider them simply because they extend beyond the limits of reason alone; he called it abolishing knowledge in order to increase faith. Because Kant located the divine Being in reason separate from man, and not in man as Liberal Protestantism would locate him, Ludwig Feuerbach actually classified him and even Fichte and Hegel as residual supernaturalists.[25]

At this point a bold line separates Liberalism from Kantianism, even though Ritschl and Harnack relied on the naturalism, or at least anti-metaphysicalism, of Kantian language to work their way around blatantly romantic systems back to the Enlightenment.[26] The Liberal will not drop the inconceivable

---

[23]Ibid., p. 65.
[24]Ibid., p. 66.
[25]*PTNC*, p. 535.
[26]Ibid., p. 655.

incompatibilities, but insists on making them comprehensible by reducing them to natural configurations, conformed to plausible human terms, and contemptuous of mysteries presuming upon theory. Harnack's account of what the Reformation accomplished reads like the description of the domestication of a chimpanzee: "Religion was taken out of the vast and monstrous fabric which had been previously called by its name — a fabric embracing the Gospel and holy water, the priesthood of all believers and the Pope on his throne, Christ the Redeemer and St. Anne — and was *reduced* to its essential factors, to the Word of God and to faith."[27]

In support, Vidler likens the reduction to losing weight, which results in improved health. But the plain fact is that Harnack's reductionism is by way of dismemberment, the kind of weight loss induced by amputation. Thus his case for removing the Fourth Gospel altogether: it "cannot be taken as an historical authority in the ordinary meaning of the word. The author of it acted with sovereign freedom, transposed events and put them in a strange light, drew up the discourses himself, and illustrated great thoughts by imaginary situations . . ."[28]

Sixty years earlier he might have reasoned out a theory to which Christianity must conform; but now, he says, we must use psychological analysis, taking care not to confuse such with a wrongful mixture of apologetic method and scientific history.[29] Little wonder is it, then, that the Catholic Modernist Alfred Loisy challenged Harnack's description of himself as an historian and not a theologian. Harnack had not studied Christ as an historical phenomenon; he had viewed Christ telescopically through his teaching of trust in God as Father, and to this he had subordinated the Messianic discourses and eschatological warnings. There is logic in the umbrage taken by the Modernists at the Liberal Protestant subjectivization of Christology by their

---

[27]*WIC*, p. 269.
[28]Ibid., p. 19. Cf. *TCDF*, p. 18.
[29]Ibid., pp. 6, 9.

misinterpretation of the *entos humon* in Luke 17:21: "... the Kingdom of God is within you." The Modernist reaction to the Liberals was in effect a case of idealism scoring off winded heirs of rationalism. George Tyrrell wrote archly for the Modernist side: "The Church that Harnack sees looking back through nineteen centuries of Catholic darkness, is only the reflection of a Liberal Protestant face, seen at the bottom of a deep well."[30] Or, as Newman might have put it, at the bottom of a shallow well. His *Grammar* quotes a riposte to the admirer who had said Hume was a clear thinker: "Shallows are clear."[31] The Modernist complaint could not have been about the Liberal's naturalism; what really annoyed the Modernist was the Liberal's rationalistic optimism which refused to acknowledge the "incurable tragedy" of human life. As despair is an offence against the theological virtue of hope, so is optimism, as it presumes the adequacy of human agency. As the Modernists offended from the side of the former, the Liberals offended by their presumption; it took one culprit to detect the other. Harnack's optimistic counterfeit of hope shows how intemperate flight from blind faith must conclude, not in a perceptive faith available to reason but in a bland intuition. The Modernist could detect that only because he had made the same mistake a different way.

It is true that Kant, much as any Liberal Protestant, had portrayed Christ essentially as the model of moral perfectibility. He said perfectibility, and not perfection, because all are still progressing toward the perfect state; and the Christ of Kant is not an archetype inasmuch as he is the substantial encouragement for attaining to some archetypal status. A century before Harnack, Herder could combine an intuitive attraction to the model of Jesus as a Platonic recollection, with a moral utilitarianism characteristic of the Enlightenment. In

---

[30]George Tyrrell, *Christianity at the Cross-Roads* (London: 1909), p. 49.

[31]John Henry Newman, *An Essay in Aid of a Grammar of Assent* (London: 1870), p. 47.

consort, the Christ of Harnack "has as yet yielded to no
man . . ."[32]   If the Arians of the fourth century had made a
diphthong their creed, Harnack is sub-Arian by his confession "as
yet" in that line.   And again, his support is more impulsive than
critical: "Most of us regard this identification (of the Logos with
Christ) as inadmissible, because the way in which we conceive the
world and ethics does not point to the existence of any logos at
all."[33]   With a dogmatic ferocity possible only in one who has
abolished all dogmas, he dates the equation of Logos with Jesus
Christ to about the year 130; and yet a few years after these
lectures, he will stun his colleagues with early dates for the
Synoptics and Acts.   But the chief point, uncomfortably as the
Liberal would receive it, is the obvious commitment to a
philosophical pre-supposition, removing faith from objective
historical allusion. There is an added defensiveness, therefore, in
Harnack's description of himself as an historian. But an historian
he was, and probably his age's finest archeologist of pre-Nicene
texts, his conclusions notwithstanding (even if this is like saying
with the muse that Wagner's music is not as bad as it sounds).

Ideological appropriation of historical items is precisely
what Harnack had repudiated as un-scientific. "The Bible and
only the Bible" becomes an absolutist and anti-historical slogan
which, by its anthropological subjectivism if not by its high piety,
marked it of the Enlightenment. The historian F. C. Baur (1782-
1860), himself of Hegelian sympathies, had called the rationalist
chroniclers of the previous generation "incoherent in their
estimation of facts as they worked according to an unverifiable
prejudice against the certainty of historical truth."[34]   Harnack's
rhetoric decorates his inconsistencies. Against the one assertion,
a central one of Protestant Liberalism, which finds the
hierarchical constitution bereft of primitive credentials, Harnack
speaks of a church structure highly developed and coordinated as

---

[32]*WIC*, p. 130.
[33]Ibid., p. 204.
[34]Cf. *PTNC*, p. 501.

early as the year 200.[35]   His structure, he recognizes, had
admirably vanquished polytheism, political religion and "subtle
religious philosophy" (i.e., dualism), in contradiction to his
portrayal of the official church propagating what amounted to
dualist asceticism. Kant had combined a remnant affection for
the ecclesiastical institutions which had been kind to his youth,
with contempt for clerical intelligence; Harnack respects the
intelligence of clerics but reviles their structures. And thus, with
a wistfulness unknown to Kant, Harnack seeks the primitive and
pristine Gospel brotherhood with the reverence of Rousseau in
confident quest of the Noble Savage.

As the Modernist objects, the Liberal Protestant does not
question the optimistic moral tradition which historical judgment
already had indicted. Moreover, he perpetuates, or recovers, the
split between the moral and natural universes which was the fatal
legacy of the Enlightenment. Yet he also acknowledges the lack
of autonomy to some degree, avoiding the innate contradiction in
Kant: namely, that man is both creature and an autonomous
moral agent. His theodicy is incomplete and reduced to myth;
but he does affirm the Gospel's account of ontic evil:

> Jesus, like all those of his own nation who were really in
> earnest, was profoundly conscious of the great anti-thesis
> between the kingdom of God and that kingdom of the world
> in which he saw the reign of evil and the evil one. This was
> no mere image or empty idea; it was a truth which he saw
> and felt most vividly. He was certain, then, that the
> kingdom of the world must perish and be destroyed. But
> nothing short of a battle can effect it. With dramatic
> intensity battle and victory stand like a picture before his
> soul, drawn in those large firm lines in which the prophets
> had seen them.[36]

He would not shrink this into "a pale system of ethics"; but
such is what devolves in practice. He dismisses satanic imagery

---

[35]*WIC*, pp. 192-193.
[36]Ibid., p. 53.

as "unhistorical and foolish" and presents a naturalized moral eschatology as the "special and individual" contribution of Jesus on the subject. "The kingdom of God comes by coming to the individual, by entering into his soul and laying hold of it ... God himself is the kingdom. It is not a question of angels and devils, thrones and principalities, but of God and the soul, the soul and its God."[37] Then the inclusive significance of Jesus is sloganized: "Eternal light came in and made the world look new."[38] And the word "look" is not causal or ill-chosen in this effusive poesie. We have been given an event of moral persuasiveness, not genuinely ontological, in which good and evil are shades of a moral complexion and other than the decibels of an historic cataclysm. What apophatic elements remain, are relegated to the place of accidents by the power of pure theology, by whose instrumentality false religion is cast aside. In the context of essential Christianity, the three themes of which have been given, the moral consequences follow a pattern:

> (1) Jesus was, as we have seen, steeped in the conviction that God does justice; in the end, therefore, the oppressor will not prevail, but the oppressed will get his rights.

> (2) Earthly rights are in themselves of little account, and it does not much matter if we lose them.

> (3) The world is in such an unhappy state, injustice had got so much the upper hand in it, that the victim of oppression is incapable of making good his rights even if he tries.

> (4) As God — and this is the main point — mingles His justice with mercy, and lets His sun shine on the just and on the unjust, so Jesus's disciple is to show love to his enemies and disarm them by gentleness.

The moral revolution sustains what moral people have long believed; the novelty of the Gospel is not its uniqueness but its

---

[37]Ibid., p. 56.
[38]Ibid., p. 62.

purity and strength which is conspicuous against the background
of failed religiosity and cultism.[39] Jesus is a moral beacon left
glowing in the twilight of the gods.

Scratching the Modern Man

A brief sketch, innocent of the flourish which Harnack
summons, may at least stimulate some curiosity about why he said
what he did. What happened in his generation or in the culture
of his age, to make exegesis of the supernatural indigestible to
the modern appetite? Or, what caused the brooding assumptions
which came to be called "secularism" and the "modern outlook,"
and even "post-Christianity?" What was new in the climate
which, once breathed, could dismiss anything supernaturally
connoted as "unhistorical and foolish"? The very vacuum which
rationalism had set between moral and natural realities
paradoxically electrified the cultural air. And in the way of
vacuums, it subsumed anything weaker to itself. We have come
to take it for granted and can be gratuitous when forced to speak
of it. Vidler writes, "I can see what is meant by the secularization
of the modern world and that it is an epoch-making kind of
discovery."[40] The tautology has become almost imperceptible:
how can the world be secularized, or "made itself," if it is a
creature? Such would be like divinizing God. And if
secularization claims, as it generally does, to redefine the
meaning of all history, becoming its culmination rather the way
Hegel intended his own thought to be, does it not deny itself by
just making one more epoch in the history of meaning? And if it
is a matter of the world being true to itself at long last, behaving
according to its nature, should this not be a manifestation rather
than a discovery? An advocate like Vidler does not resolve the

---

[39]Ibid., p. 48.
[40]*TCDF*, pp. 120-121.

difficulty; and by accepting the difficulty as an inspiration, he attaches to it. The title of his book is *Twentieth Century Defenders of the Faith*; it is more accurately *Twentieth Century Defenders of the Twentieth Century*. And such a battle lasts only a hundred years.

We risk word-play; but it is not play to distinguish between secularism and secularization. Secularization is the making of naturalism into the only reference of value. Secularism, which is what lies at the heart of the Liberal Protestant attempt to convince a secularized society, is a secularization of God (through rationalism) and a divinization of the world (through romanticism, which has the potential for both atheism and pantheism). Secularism is a bias so blatant that it seems incontestably objective, in the order of making a lie big enough to be believable. It comes to theology through three influences, at least: solipsism, or anthropological subjectivism; scientism, or the attribution of philosophical authority to physical formulas; and criticism, or the mythopoeic interpretation of Scripture. This came to the Liberal Protestant unconsciously as a cultural intuition; he would not have thought himself a secularist. But he had so imbued its atmosphere that he assumed Christianity could be updated by being uprooted from its metaphysics, and still be Christian.

Now while each of these influences can be expressions of the dogmatic empiricist, together they form the grand cultural tide known as romanticism, a form of what Winston Churchill in a quite different context called the refinement of unreason. Matthew Arnold, who could have worshipped Harnack's way, is the poetic model of the secularized soul watching the withdrawal of faith; but this is also prelude to an incoming wave of another system of conceptualization, and Arnold's melancholy at the parting roar is prototypically romantic. He described religion as morality "touched by emotion," a caricature which could function as a scientific diagram only for the romantic imagination. Arnold's sturdy public image does not make him any less emotive

or emoting than, say, Chateaubriand. The romantic bond
between contrasting spirits was also what helped energize the
conflict between Kingsley and Newman.[41]

Karl Barth says you only have to scratch the modern man to
discover the romantic. The term "modern" is plastic enough, but
"romantic" is perplexingly more so. Barth never seems so
romantic himself, and uncharacteristically vague, then when he
tries to define it. He is convinced, though, that as a reaction to
the Enlightenment, romanticism is not so profound as Kant, or
radical as Hegel, or mature as Goethe, but it is far more inclusive
than any of them as a cultural phenomenon. Romanticism
combines psychologism and historicism; a synthesis of love for a
foreign object and love received from that object; an inescapable
yearning; and a desire to hymn the splendors of creation while
harboring an unspoken feeling that "the miracle of created life"
is "identical with the secret of the Creator." By raising emotion
to the dignity of thought, romanticism cast a tremendous burden
on the future of the intellect.

The theatricality of Harnack's lectures are a kinetic example
of the intellect struggling in the new equation of the sensual and
the intellectual. True, he abuses the romantic aesthete, but again
the posturing is defensive. We have mentioned Rousseau.
Harnack's fantasies of what constitutes primitive Christianity
makes him a closer cousin to Chateaubriand whom he mocks
"standing before the ancient ruins of the Church and exclaiming:
'How beautiful!' "[42] Verses of the young yet representative
romantic theologian Friedrich von Hardenberg, called Novalis,
(1772-1801) could supply a century later for Harnack's
"unadulterated" Gospel to which the apostles themselves had
scarce access:

---

[41]Cf. F. H. Bradley, *Ethical Studies*, p. 281, in Bernard M. G.
Reardon, *From Coleridge to Gore* (London: 1971), p. 394fn.
[42]*WIC*, p. 199. On romanticism, cf. *PTNC*, p. 348.

What seek we in this world below
With all our love and duty?
The old is worthless, let it go!
How shall the new bring beauty?
O sad, forlorn and out of time
Who warmly love the golden Prime.

The golden Prime, when senses light
In upward flames were glowing;
When men the Father's hand and sight
Felt, his own presence knowing;
When high and simple thought was rife,
And time showed forth the perfect life.[43]

Poetry is a way of "pleasantly surprising art, of making an object strange, and yet familiar and attractive"; Novalis approaches a definition of the aesthetic not unsympathetic to what in our moment is named, for want of a better term, as post-modern culture.[44] Post-modernism is only a little less capable of precise description than is romanticism. Yet both attempt a general cultural synthesis of language, philosophy, art and nature, a synthesis which transcends the materialist propaedeutic of rationalism on the one hand and the bankrupt modern confidence in psychologism and historicism on the other.

Barth's critical mind can be seen in the philosophical art by which Novalis bridged the eighteenth and nineteenth centuries, a permanent quality of romantic imagination which outlived the romantic era itself. So one might also consider the possibility of a neo-romanticism capable of spanning the twentieth and twenty-first centuries, renewing sensitivity to authentic history and imagination in an appeal against determinism and subjectivism, both of which have been the infection of modernity. But such sensitivity was not conspicuous in Harnack. The romanticism of his diction yielded primacy of place to the rationalism of his method. The combination was volatile, a romanticism without

---

[43]"Hymns to the Night" in *PTNC*, pp. 356-357.
[44]In *PTNC*, p. 351.

grace and a rationalism without reserve. At moments it made his discourse even brutal in its lack of logic and its docility to the groundless cliché: "... we know that the Gospel came from a time in which the marvellous may be said to have been something of a daily occurrence ... No one can feel anything to be an interruption of the order of Nature who does not yet know what the order of Nature is ... we are firmly convinced that what happens in space and time is subject to the general laws of motion, and that in this sense, as an interruption of the order of Nature, there can be no such thing as 'miracles'."[45]

Once miracles are confined to "the ability to escape from the power and the service of transitory things," supernatural power in any form takes on the connotation of the superhuman.[46] Inevitably, a nostalgic superhumanism proposes itself as a replacement for Christology; and if that was not an intention of Liberalism, it became the content of much preaching in its wake. This writer once heard a New York preacher say that if Mozart could compose a sonata at the age of seven, Jesus surely could have ascended to heaven at the age of thirty-three. Harnack would have been appalled, but he was nonetheless the formal agent of such a muddle.

As romanticism may be detected behind his attempt to reconcile the Gospel and nature, so may it also have been influential in his cavalier use of logic. In reaction to the credulous for whom the universe is a cornucopia of miracles, do the incredulous become more trustworthy the less they find miracles anywhere? Harnack was working with a form criticism and cosmogony crude in shape and incapable of serving him well. It seems never to have occurred to him, as it did to Alfred North Whitehead, that faith in scientific development can be traced to the scholasticism which Harnack considered the epitome of

---

[45]*WIC*, pp. 24, 25, 26.
[46]Ibid., p. 26.

ignorance.[47] The purer romanticism of Novalis, who was born the same year that Töllner made his poignant deathbed profession, wove the New Testament miracles into a gossamer poetry, even trying to restore the Virgin Mary to the Protestant economy of nature and grace; Harnack must smash them as violently as Kant smashes the atonement itself as a contradiction of autonomy.

A sense of impatience pervades these sixteen lectures of Harnack, and not the impatience of anticipation found in Schleiermacher at the beginning of the Liberal presence. There is an almost desperate attempt, a last-ditch struggle, to persuade, hence the fulminations against intransigent priests of an obscurantist church. Once again Barth encapsulates the anomie: "The century had become tired and somehow sad for all its enforced jollity. The age of Hegel and the age of the superseding of Hegel are related as is the battle of Sedan to the battle of the Marne. This time, too, there was an abundance of victorious bulletins, but something had gone wrong at the top, and there was a premonition that things would turn out badly."[48] The restlessness evidently moved the dubious Catholics away from Liberal enticements toward a more intuitive romance of their own in the form of progressive idealism, "legitimizing" their own course by showing the failure of the Protestants along the way. And in spite of this, they could not persuade the world that they were the last and best expression of Catholicism, no more than Harnack was the full fruition of Lutheranism.

The Modernists, aided by the efforts of revisionist biographers like Henri Bremond, applied Newman's theory of the development of doctrine to their own ends, as Harnack had appropriated Luther on justification, but the results were whole new puzzles. Vidler sees some sort of inventiveness in the way Loisy and Tyrrell apply Newman's argument in a way Newman never meant. But to countenance that is a theological form of

---

[47]Cf. Eric Mascall, *The Secularization of Christianity* (London: 1965), p. 194.

[48]*PTNC*, p. 387.

deconstruction, like using a parable to assert an opposite maxim, or invoking the Fourth Gospel to silence the Logos. Harnack was not so byzantine. When he met an inconvenient contradiction he just cut it out.

One trait seems common among reductionists of every school, if it is not unfeeling to say so, and that is a fraternal bond of condescension. In each instance, and exceptions are to be found only by the meticulous, the author appeals to the superior intelligence of his audience. He suggests that the reordering of belief to meet the common needs of common folk is understood only by uncommon minds. The populist in religion is not without his support, but it rarely includes the people. Vidler made a dated case for Liberal Protestantism having done "much more than any other version of Christian faith to enable ordinary people — as distinguished from sophisticated theologians — to continue to be professing Christians."[49] Absent is any possibility of sophisticated people and ordinary theologians. And he overlooks the forthright way Liberal Protestants themselves described their duty to the privileged.

For example, Bultmann claims that *What is Christianity?* demonstrates what forms of Christianity may be "current among the broad circles of the educated and semi-educated laymen to whom (the Liberal) must address his sermons and teachings."[50] Matthew Arnold's darlings were those who are "won to the modern spirit by habits of intellectual seriousness." Their habits apparently become vices, for they "cannot receive what sets these habits at naught, and will not try to force themselves to do so," though they are numbered among those who "have stood near enough to the Christian religion to feel the attraction which a thing so very great, when one stands really near to it, cannot but

---

[49]*TCDF*, p. 12.
[50]Introduction to *WIC* (Harper Torchbooks edition, New York: 1957). Cf. *TCDF*, p. 13.

exercise, and who have familiarity with the Bible and some practice in using it."[51]

Professor William Sanday, who wrote a generous study of *What is Christianity?* in England, reminded readers in another context that the Savior reaches out to the cultivated quite as he does the simple.[52] This truth needs restatement ever more strongly now than ever; the question is whether the Savior hands the cultivated an edited Gospel. Harnack was intent on simplifying the complicated religion of simple people for complicated people. Newman had believed, perhaps innocently, that his *Grammar* would appeal to the general reader; he goes over the heads of his audience only because he has an exalted opinion of them, an opinion which is in fact a self-projection. "Again and again, one feels, when he is speaking on man in general he really is alluding to one very unusual man — himself."[53] It is true that he reserves the Illative Sense, or speeded-up inference, to "gifted . . . or educated . . . or otherwise well-prepared minds . . ."[54] And he may have been mistaken to think it exclusively as an individual endowment without heeding the collective reasoning of the human race. Elsewhere he recalls Augustine: "Securus iudicat orbis terrarum." But his impulse is a genuine aristocratic respect for the common man free of the Liberal's condescending spirit. If Newman is donnish he is nobly so, and a world apart from the bourgeois didacticism of the Liberal lecture halls. Many of his Birmingham lectures were delivered to young mill hands after their day's work. While the reader may wonder what their impressions were (evidently the *Lectures on the Prophetical Office of the Church* given at the Corn Exchange got laughs at the right places), Newman had every

---

[51]Matthew Arnold, *God and the Bible*, Preface, p. xxiii. Cf. Reardon, op. cit., p. 384.

[52]William Sanday, *Bishop Gore's Challenge to Criticism* (London: 1914), pp. 30-31.

[53]Reardon, op. cit., p. 144.

[54]Newman, op. cit., p. 361.

expectation of being understood, and that may have made the greatest impression of all. With a passion of his own, Harnack addressed modern souls; Newman addressed immortal souls.

Antecedent judgment, or presumption, characterizes faith; and Newman was certain that holiness, surpassing erudition, is the guarantee against faith surrendering to superstition. Holiness is the "quickening and illuminating principle of true faith, giving it eyes, hands, and feet."[55] In scholastic idiom this is *fides formata caritate*, which Luther's *fides informis* denuded to a bare act of mind without intrinsic moral content. The Liberal Protestant dedication to moral evidences may have been by way of reaction to what Luther left out. Harnack frequently speaks of "light and warmth" one way or another; but, devoid of supernatural agency, they are not as Newman meant them, as evidence of supernatural grace. Thus Wilfrid Ward could say that the Oxford school generally wrote about religious knowledge, and the Liberals were occupied with the science of evidence. To Newman's way of thinking, Liberalism in England stood for the "anti-dogmatic principle," even though the Liberalism of which he spoke was outright secular humanism with none of Liberal Protestantism's claims on religion. That of course applies to Harnack as well. He would have considered Newman's theology apologetical and, therefore, not scientific in its insistence on the inability of reason apart from faith to resolve doubt as certitude.[56]

The rationalist quest for a certifiable, or historical, Jesus, becomes an epic truly romantic in its yearning which energizes itself by its very incompleteness. Yet the rationalist prejudice insists that it is complete even when the divine Christ, the mystical Church and the efficacious Sacraments are missing.

---

[55]Newman, *Fifteen Sermons Preached before the University of Oxford* (London: 1871), p. 216.

[56]Wilfrid Ward, *William G. Ward and the Oxford Movement* (London: 1889), I. 392.

The description of himself as the Son of God, Messianic though it may have been in its original conception, lies very much nearer to our modern way of thinking than the other, for Jesus himself gave a meaning to this conception which almost takes it out of the class of Messianic ideas, or at all events does not make its inclusion in that class necessary to a proper understanding of it. On the other hand, if we do not desire to be put off with a lifeless word, the description of himself as the Messiah is at first blush one that is quite foreign to our ideas. Without some explanation we cannot understand, nay, unless we are Jews we cannot understand at all, what this post of honour means and what rank and character it possesses. It is only when we have ascertained its meaning by historical research that we can ask whether the word has a significance which in any way survives the destruction of the husk in which it took shape in Jewish political life.[57]

Messiahship can be dispatched summarily without difficulty once it has been flattened into a "post of honour." So casual a definition in a Patristics scholar is unsettling. "Son of God," rightly understood according to Harnack, "means nothing but the knowledge of God."[58] Now nothing could be more radical and astonishing than such knowledge, but here Harnack insists the discussion "must stop." He is not being mystical in his reserve; that is not his style. Given his boldness in other contexts, the arrest of speculation is disingenuous. But his testiness may spring from knowing that he is not dealing with light matters. Again, "If the resurrection meant nothing but that a deceased body of flesh and blood came to life again, we should make short work of this tradition." Even if the resurrection meant nothing but that, and was proved to be that, Harnack would have had to cancel his next lecture. He dismisses the whole doctrine as "paradoxical" and "incredible." And again one must insist: paradoxical does not mean impossible, and credibility pertains to certainty and not certitude, as Newman was at pains to show.

---

[57]*WIC*, p. 127.
[58]Ibid., p. 128.

At this point, Harnack exegetes beneath his capabilities. As
Kant had used John 3:8 as a proof text for de-mythologization,
Harnack makes gymnastic use of John 20:29 to argue for an
unhistorical resurrection: "Blessed are they that have not seen
and have yet believed." The case is closed tersely: "This grace
was the birthplace of the destructible belief that death is
vanquished, that there is a life eternal."[59] Now a grave which
becomes a birthplace is from any angle a remarkable thing. So
the New Testament focuses on the historical details surrounding
it: the calling of Mary's name in the garden, the description of
the tomb itself, the encounter on the Emmaus road, the gesture
to Thomas, the one hundred and fifty-three fish caught, and the
"more than five hundred witnesses" cited by St. Paul. But all this
is lost on Harnack for whom "there is no tradition of single
events which is quite trustworthy."[60]

In friendly estimation, Liberal Protestants were right to
formulate the doctrine of Christ's person as an expression of
believers "who had been brought into communion with God
through Jesus Christ."[61] But they lapse into convolutions when
they say that this assertion is not a speculative dogma which has
to be accepted on authority. If a dogma is accepted on authority
it is no longer speculative, and if it is not speculative it properly
belongs to revelation. Indeed, it is dogma by having been
revealed. The Liberal makes a dogma speculative by making it
exclusively experiential, but this syllogism eludes Harnack. His
Gospel has "only one aim — the finding of the living God, the
finding of Him by every individual as *his* God ..."[62] As an
argument, it is too impatient to be theological, and too vague to
be philosophical. It becomes theosophy by another name, and
Harnack's euphemism for that is history. His favorable glances

---

[59]Ibid., p. 162.
[60]Ibid.
[61]*TCDF*, p. 66.
[62]*WIC*, p. 199.

towards Pietism bear this out, for they are attracted not by the doctrine in it but rather by the doctrine that is not in it.

In such a system, St. Francis of Assisi and Newton are exhibited together as embodiments of the "higher righteousness" of which Christ is the forerunner.[63] Given their mutual respect for doctrine, St. Francis and Sir Isaac would have been happier with each other than either would have been with Harnack. Perhaps Harnack had himself in mind when he told of an "inconvenient theologian" whom someone wanted removed to the philosophy faculty, "for then instead of an unbelieving theologian we should have a believing philosopher."[64] As it was, no theological movement sought more intensely than did Liberal Protestantism to appeal in the vernacular in order to convert the modern sceptic to some para-Christian form. Yet, though its appeal has not totally vanished, it is in a delicate state as attests the hemorrhaging membership of the mainline Protestant churches who gave it a once-fashionable home. In the United States, for example, in less than twenty-five years since 1965, the Presbyterian Church lost 25% of its members and the Episcopal Church lost 28%. Apologists will nonetheless insist that the reductionist approach has been demanded by some sort of cultural plebiscite. The truth is, the spirit of Liberalism has been an esoteric attempt to commandeer the masses and subject them to an artificial philosophy of the state as teacher in place of God.

Because the magisterial force of Christianity has been universally functional only in Catholicism, the spirit of Liberalism is intrinsically an anti-Catholic spirit. This was true in Harnack's day as now: at the height of the Bismarckian *Kulturkampf*, 989 Catholic parishes were deprived of priests. Harnack's pretensions to social consciousness failed him in 1876, when at the eager age of twenty-five, he made no objection to the imprisonment or exile of every Catholic bishop in Prussia.

---

[63]Ibid., p. 298.
[64]Ibid., p. 294.

Harnack's later contempt for the claims of the Catholic Church, like that of later Liberals, was certainly not unaffected by an attempt to justify his own moral surrender to statism as a new Messiahship, and to the state as the vicariate of God, and to the passing philosophical mood as the climate of heaven. The Church, then, can be tolerated only as a collective: the People of God yes, but the Body of Christ no. What the Liberal dismissed as triumphalism when Rome spoke was prophecy from the lips of professors appointed by the bureaucracy in Berlin.

For all its accommodations to scepticism, the ones with whom Liberalism has had the least success have been the modern sceptics themselves. It prospered better as shop talk among theologians and as the remnant allusion of the Western bourgeoisie easing out of Christianity, and its optimistic cadences only disintegrated when much of the twentieth century blew up. The children of the age may be wiser but only in their own day; and a day lasts no more than a day. The Liberal Protestant version of the Gospel was prophetic solely in the sense that it was a form of self-destruction which, with sober consistency and stalwart aplomb, destroyed itself.

Tyrrell on Liberalism and Modernism

The Modernist Crusade

In well known words which have offended those to whom they were directed, Pope Pius X called Catholic Modernism the synthesis of all heresies. To digest Modernism's varied forms is too large a task for an essay, even an essay relieved of scientific research in asserting its opinions. The Pontiff was prepared for the test of time; after all, that is why he published his verdict. Even his critics must admit that he had no intention, as he accused the Modernists of having, of separating theological and pastoral exegesis from scientific and historical exegesis. George Tyrrell (1861-1909) was every whit as prepared for the verdict of history, and made his dying prayer a higher plea: "I am glad God is going to judge me, and not any of his servants."[1] At least from the remove of these few years and from the evidence of this most poignant of protagonists, it is possible to attempt to approach one of the issues in the debate, and the one surely at the heart of it: Was Catholic Modernism Catholic?

Rome had seen inconsistency, and even insincerity, in the Modernists' method. What they preached and what they thought were not appreciably the same. Today the accusation is made another way when it is asked why do not the heterodox descendants of the original Modernists simply part from the Church the way they used to? The answer is that they did not

---

[1] *George Tyrrell's Letters*, ed. Maude D. Petre (London: 1920), p. 301, hereafter *Letters*.

used to. Alfred Loisy (1857-1919) and Tyrrell were separated from the Church only reluctantly, though Tyrrell did not die the apostate Loisy became. Baron von Hügel never left in piety and gradually made himself more secure doctrinally, perhaps risking the virtue of friendship in the exercise of diplomacy. Only minor figures like the American Paulist, William L. Sullivan (1872-1935) voluntarily left, he for Unitarianism. The Modernist bear only went into hibernation after its condemnation in the encyclical "Pascendi Dominici Gregis," nurtured on grievance, and emerged larger in its present phase. At the height of its first phase, which is the subject of consideration here, the theological treatises were followed by a rash of novels seeking to show that Modernism was the new way to be Catholic. Their authors tended to be distant friends of the Muse; but then *Loss and Gain* and *Fabiola* did not establish the reputations of Newman and Wiseman either. Literary energy outran talent only slightly less than it does in the potboiling Catholic novelists of today: back then there were Sullivan's *The Priest* (1911) and Gerald O'Donovan's *Father Ralph* (1914). Responding authors, like Paul Bourget who wrote an anti-Modernist "salad of Modernism and adultery" called *Le Demon de Midi* (1914) set a standard which has not been neglected since.

The Modernists would not leave the Church willingly, even when they allowed the bromide which says the Church left them. They could not flourish without the Church, and every essay or theological tract or novel was obsessed with the dark Roman shadow. This was so even when they were rusticated by the ecclesiastical system which they were trying to marry to modern culture. In 1869 Tyrrell inscribed his Breviary: "Thou shalt see from afar the land which the Lord God will give to the children of Israel, but thou shalt not enter therein." (Deut. 32:52) His first inconsistency may have been his attempt to make a home for all humanity in the Church which he considered a cultural exile. Liberal Protestantism had the same purpose in mind, but the tension between Liberal Protestantism and Catholic Modernism was the sort which exercises people of different stations caught in the same lifeboat. The Modernists had tried to save the ship, and the Liberals had torpedoed her; and their joint anxiety became unbearable when they saw the ship sailing on, almost blithely. The Catholic Modernists and the Liberal Protestant only spoke to each other to say the ship would go over the edge nonetheless. The Pope wrote "Pascendi Dominici Gregis" as his way of saying that the world is round.

Tyrrell's entire literary output occupied but a dozen years, from the *Nova et Vetera* of 1897 to the dramatic *Christianity at the Crossroads* in 1909, the manuscript lying on the desk of the room in which he died. He suffered from Bright's disease and its nervous depredations, but he made no excuses. He said that he meant what he wrote, and it would be patronizing to discount that. Yet the unedifying rancor which increases with the years jars with the detachment of his youthful dedication. Too quickly in a short life does the razor of, say, his 1899 Oxford lectures become a sledgehammer against Cardinal Mercier in 1908. The most venomous polemic is sadder than Harnack's pompous bombast. The Catholic Modernists took themselves no less seriously than did the Liberal Protestants. And the onus on the Liberal pride, which thinks God is smaller than he is, does not outweigh that on the Modernist pride, which thinks he should be bigger.

Tyrrell cared for Catholic Christianity "more as a life, and less merely as a truth."[2] The thought was inconceivable to a Liberal Protestant husking the Gospel for the hidden kernel of truth which would furnish the inclusive diet of the intellect. Through Harnack's spectacles the *quid inde* of historicism is that it attains to a verbal disclosure of that truth. But all such is misspent energy so far as the Modernists measure the case, for Jesus Christ imparts no truth that is not a spirit. There is no absolute

---

[2]*Autobiography and Life of George Tyrrell* Vol. I (London: 1912), p. 119.

essence of Christianity or of Christianity's Gospel; Loisy and Tyrrell and their company saw no point in looking for the kernel, no more than in looking for the whole stalk. What gives the growth is what counts. Doctrines are not accidentally reformulated; they are changed, and God is far more than the granter of truth for he is the Life of truth. Surely there is no truth for living more vital than the living of the truth. It is quixotic to "go back" with the Ritschlians to an essence. And as for Harnack's encapsulation of the Fatherhood of God, Tyrrell satirized it as "Christianity in a nutshell."[3] Satire indeed was the Modernist's grammar, and it spared no invective in its own encapsulation of Liberalism: "The Pearl of Great Price fell into the dustheap of Catholicism, not without the wise permission of Providence, desirous to preserve it till the day when Germany should rediscover it and separate it from its useful but deplorable accretions."[4] That way of patronizing Liberal paternalism had a confidence which in an unguarded moment one might actually take for the preaching of Peter and Paul, and it might well have been their preaching had they been European wits instead of Jewish apostles.

The Liberal-Modernist Dialogue

From the Protestant side, Baur and the Tübingen school had examined Catholicism and found a synthesis of Jewish and Gentile Christianities. Harnack had sympathized with any attempt to prove the derivative nature of the Church, but he decided that it must only be the fancy of Hellenism, on the grounds that Jewish Christianity amounted to little by the second century. Rudolf Sohm had joined the fray, dating Catholicism to

---

[3]George Tyrrell, *Through Scylla and Charybdis: or The Old Theology and the New* (London: 1907), p. 36, hereafter *Scylla and Charybdis*.

[4]George Tyrrell, *Christianity at the Cross-Roads* (London: 1909).

the transformation from charism to institutionalism in the late first century. Where Harnack had seen the elegant hand of Greek at work, Sohm had seen the heavier hand of Roman law. But they agreed that the hands were of a magician. Harnack thought Sohm's concentration obscured the dominant role of tradition as the stultifier of the charismatic Gospel, but they both saw Catholicism as a trick done with smoke and mirrors. What they called a trick the Catholic Modernists were not ashamed to call a sacred tradition which was nothing less than the life of faith itself.

Intolerant as he was of Harnack and Sohm, Tyrrell was rather fascinated with what he considered the more facile syncretism of Sabatier: Catholicism was not bankrupt, but it was the second of four phases in Christian evolution, the first having been Jewish Messianism, the third Protestantism, and the future fourth a pure religion of the soul's filial relationship with God. Only the final development could realize that transcendent moral purity which arbitrary authority had impeded, both in Catholic ecclesiasticism and Protestant biblicism. A mediocre historian himself, the early Tyrrell dismissed Sabatier's full scheme, but studied its progressive hope, so much more vital and amenable than was Harnack's essentialism to the Catholic concept of development.

The abidingly cynical Anglican Dean Inge, like Tyrrell, thought that Liberal criticism as a whole replaced one invention with another, and that Harnack's re-fabrication of primitive Christianity was, as we might put it, about as authentic as a religious epic by Cecil B. DeMille. It is not "really natural for faith to represent its ideas in the form of historical facts when it knows that these facts have no historical basis."[5] Or, as Tyrrell insisted, historical criticism is not historical when it tries "getting at the more inward and deeper truth through the husk of the

---

[5]William Ralph Inge, *Outspoken Essays* (London: 1920), p. 161.

phenomenal and relative."[6]   But Tyrrell lacked professional equipment; he was less a biblical critic than an historian, and his literary executor would regret that he so occupied himself with historical criticism at which he was much the amateur.[7]

Tyrrell's formation had been eclectic, grabbing at authors here and there, sometimes inspired solely by private inclination and not infrequently urged on by von Hügel, who enjoyed watching the energetic, and even brilliant, young mind light up with a new source or a novel system. But when each firefly died in the bottle, Tyrrell kept trying to resuscitate it long after von Hügel had meandered off to another diversion.

Earlier explorations had brought him face to face with a purported rationalism which frustrated his Catholic obligations. "I have been reading Harnack — in English, of course — and have been impressed with the madness of supposing that we can go on ignoring so plain a fact as the growth of Catholicism out of a germ as unlike Catholicism as a walnut is unlike a tree ... and yet our theologians go on dreaming and romancing about a full-fledged apostolic Catholicism, and are anxious to anathematize the very notion of development by putting Newman's *Essay* on the Index."[8]   That Rome had resisted any such urgings, and that St. Pius X would reiterate in the *Acta* Newman's importance for right development theory, was irrelevant to incipient hysteria. In November 1907 Tyrrell urged Canon Alfred Lilley to inform "The Times" that the Pope had condemned Newman *ipso facto* in "Pascendi."[9]   His imaginings were easily stirred by the Liberal Protestants who seemed to be scoring well, though for the other side. Disagreeable as their anti-Catholic polemicism was, it did cast a glaring light on what appeared ever more to Tyrrell like

---

[6]*Scylla and Charybdis*, op. cit., p. 302.

[7]Cf. Maude Petre, *Von Hügel and Tyrrell: The Story of a Friendship* (London: 1937), pp. 118-120.

[8]*Letters* (to von Hügel, June 16, 1900), p. 79.

[9]Vid. Alec Vidler, *A Variety of Catholic Modernists* (Cambridge: 1970), p. 156, hereafter *Vidler*.

motley decay. The ossification, to his psychological taste, was deadliest in the form of arbitrary authoritarianism. The more he came to think himself abused and neglected by it, the more the probing light hurt; but he would rather aim it himself than leave it to any German sceptic with little idea of the glory missed in the glare. His method, then, must be to demonstrate how Harnack's school was uncomprehending of its target.

The most contumacious criticism comes at the end of Tyrrell's life. Churning energy would turn against the latter-day Scholastics of his own Church who once had taken sweet counsel with him and walked as friends. The Protestants should be shown Catholic minds awake. And if German critics found corruptions in some Catholic development, very well then, they should see a Catholic who could think without them: without the Scholastic doctrines of the Church and Sacraments, without ecclesiastical authority, without immutable dogma. This would paint a grand scene to move any mind connected to a heart, the sense of transcendence in which Catholicism had her chief claim to legitimacy quite as Liberal Protestantism had become counterfeit by not having it. By way of sobering enthusiasm, it would have to be said that Tyrrell's landscape of Catholic thought was its own kind of counterfeit; its transcendence appears much like the morality of the Liberal. Matthew Arnold's "morality touched by emotion" is a short semantic skip toward Tyrrell's vital immanence, which is not true mystery at all but mystification touched by emotion.

In Tyrrell appears a tendency certainly not invented by him, and one fresh in the Church's early controversies, but a tendency which has nearly become polity in modern times: and that is the anthropocentric fixation with reducing theological questions to *ad hominem* attacks, questioning motives rather than arguments. In one so neurasthenic and even feline as Tyrrell, it attained to gigantic proportions. The more fellow Catholics accuse him of a Protestantizing rationalism, the more he puts the blame on clerical authorities who would deprive the soul of divine immanence by mediating the transcendent. Defensiveness finally breaks any bonds of reserve in *Christianity at the Cross-Roads*.[10] Ultramontanists are accused of confounding the true economy of religion and reason as much as any rationalist. There is no recourse to Liberal Protestantism constituted of "a vague amiability whose roots are nowhere and its branches everywhere."[11] But Christianity was served no better by the lethargic mentality of nineteenth century pseudo-Scholastics who defied the progressive character of tradition. At least here Tyrrell was in accord with Harnack's bald conclusion: "The declaration that the empirical institutions of the Church, created for and necessary to this purpose, are apostolic, a declaration which amalgamates them with the essence and content of the Gospel and places them beyond all criticism, is the peculiarly 'Catholic' feature."[12] From George Tyrrell, then, a plague on both houses.

He surveys a field to decide where the battle must be, and begins the march, grabbing whatever weapons lie along the path. From Harnack he uncritically grabs the Hellenization theory; from Sohm the element of legal development; then he added Sabatier's phases of evolution and, most important of all, because they finally undermine the whole Liberal edifice, the eschatologism of Weiss and Schweitzer. Having read Sabatier, "I ask myself frankly, Am I implicitly a liberal Protestant, or is Sabatier a liberal Catholic? Or is there still an irreducible difference of principle between us? I believe there is, in that I regard the official 'Ecclesia Docens' not merely as 'expressing' the mind of the whole Church . . . but also as (in virtue of an implicit delegation) 'imposing' the general mind on the individual with an authority that is 'moral', and not purely intellectual, like a

---

[10]Cf. eg., *Christianity at the Cross-Roads*, p. 44.

[11]*Scylla and Charybdis*, p. 190. Cf. Gabriel Daly, *Transcendence and Immanence: A Study in Catholic Modernism and Integralism* (Oxford: 1980), p. 147.

[12]Adolf Harnack, *History of Dogma* Vol. II (London: 1900), p. 2 n. 1.

consensus of experts..." But having eaten the cake, he would have it still: "... I look on the whole body of official teaching of to-day as the public and authorised expression of the spiritual life of the faithful in its present state of development."[13] Paradoxical this is not, inconsistent it is; and thus is laid the ground of frustration which becomes an increasingly misanthropic anger and a continuum of dalliances with illogic. Creeds are "the creation of (the Church's collective mind, but guided by her collective religious experience by the spirit of Christ that is immanent in all her members."[14]

In the Encyclical "Pascendi" two years earlier, St. Pius X observed of the Modernists:

> ... in their books one finds some things which might well have been dictated by a rationalist. When they write history they make no mention of the divinity of Christ, but when they are in the pulpit they profess it clearly; again, when they are dealing with history they take no account of the Fathers and the Councils, but when they catechize the people, they cite them respectfully.

Modernists themselves did not interiorize their sense of displeasure. Six years earlier, however, Tyrrell had written to Henri Bremond, his brother Jesuit who later would enrage Loisy by taking the Oath against Modernism:

> For the time one is as an actor who sincerely forgets himself in his part; and, by repetition, this professional self comes, in our own mind, to take the place of the real... Our whole life, in the pulpit, the confessional, the chair, the parlour, forces us to play a part; to speak in the name of the Church or of the Society, or of a system and tradition which is *ours*, as our clothes are, but is not *we*. At most we are defending a

---

[13]*Letters* (February 22, 1904), p. 89.
[14]George Tyrrell, Lecture at King's College, London (March 26, 1909) in *Heythrop Journal* Vol. 12 (1971), pp. 145-146.

thesis proposed to us by another. I begin to think the only
real sin is suicide, or not being one's self.[15]

The man's own theory develops as radically as he claims the
Church's doctrine does, so the statements should be read in
context. It remains true, nonetheless, that a dozen years are not
an era and so it would be legitimate to take the latter Tyrrell as
his representative voice. By the time the thirty-first proposition
of the Syllabus "Lamentabili Sane Exitu" on July 3, 1907
condemned the denial of divine inspiration in the Pauline,
Johannine and Conciliar Christologies, Tyrrell had assumed the
Liberal Protestant line on the hypostatic union; it is a divine
influence upon the consciousness or sub-consciousness of Christ,
by which he becomes aware of the unique favor of love which
God showed towards him. With the Liberals he also held that
Christ had erred in expecting the imminent advent of the
Parousia. And they shared the distinction, expounded by Sohm,
and which would be an object of censure in Pius XII's Encyclical
Mystici Corporis, of a contradiction between external juridical
elements and interior mystical elements in the life of the Church.
Here was a pseudo-Gnostic, and no less neo-Kantian, aversion to
the "institutional Church" as some sort of impediment to
spiritual integrity; in response, the Pope said that if the
institution is an imposition, let us remember that it was imposed
by Christ. Beyond that, the atonement and priesthood of Christ
are symbolic; and in the style of Sabatier the death of Christ
figures as a martyrdom.[16] This, then, discounts the sacrificial
economy, inasmuch as martyrdom, being an act of fortitude, is
not an act of elicited *latria*.[17]

---

[15]*Letters* (September 16, 1901), p. 51. Bremond left the Jesuits in
1904; Tyrrell was dismissed in 1906.

[16]Cf. Paul Sabatier, *Modernism: The Jowett Lectures, 1968*, trans. C.
A. Miles (London: 1908); Loisy, *L'Évangile et l'Église* (Paris: 1902), ch.
3 and 4.

[17]For analysis, cf. Reginald Garrigou-Lagrange, *Christ the Saviour*
(London: 1950).

Of all the figures in the melancholy Modernist gallery, the only significant one who thought Modernism was but an elevated Liberal Protestantism was Alfred Fawkes (1850-1930), an Oratorian convert who reverted to Anglicanism.[18] Loisy wrote *L'Évangile et l'Église* to refute the notion. Tyrrell said squarely, and far more defensively than he had five years earlier when first flushed from reading Sabatier: "Whatever Jesus was, He was in no sense a Liberal Protestant. All that makes Catholicism most repugnant to present modes of thought derives from Him."[19] Yet the intensity of his repudiation is the exasperation of one man at another who, by submitting science to the bias of his own culture, has committed the same crime of his accuser.

On specifics, the Modernist could make a case. Liberalism among the Protestants was remiss in two critical areas of cultural anthropology.   First, it avoided the challenge of science by reducing Christianity to one sentiment which had no vital contact with the scientific spirit of the age.   Secondly, it appealed to history theologically but with less success historically, making it a repository to be plundered for whatever might ornament its anticipations.   Consider Loisy's telling affirmation: "Whatever we think, theologically, of tradition, whether we trust it or regard it with suspicion, we know Christ only by tradition, across tradition, and in the tradition of the primitive Christians."[20] The tradition testifies to the Church's communal experience, the characteristic of Catholicism outside of which stands the Liberals' reliance on individual experience. While clericalism is without warrant, the Church as the living tradition has a central and legitimate office of mediating revelation to God's people through her doctrine, sacraments and worship. To the end, Tyrrell was comforted by a particular devotion to the saints. Bremond recounted, in his controversial graveside eulogy, how he had repeated to his dying ears the formula: *Credo in communionem*

---

[18]Cf. *Vidler*, p. 156.
[19]*Christianity at the Cross-Roads*, p. xxi.
[20]Loisy, *L'Évangile et l'Église*, op. cit., p. 4.

sanctorum. But Harnack, as an everlasting contrast, had called the cult of the saints "Apostolico-Roman Polytheism."[21]

The contrast is understandable in view of Tyrrell's pact with the eschatologism of Weiss and Schweitzer. Christ was not a modern man preaching a modern optimism in ancient dress; he was a man of his time who knew there would be other times for which his Spirit would be the means of making the transcendent mystery of creation and redemption imminent in daily experience. But when Schweitzer eventually became a missionary doctor and Loisy retreated to raising chickens, says Gabriel Daly, "Tyrrell was still in theological harness when he died, struggling as vigorously against Liberal Protestantism as against Roman scholasticism and trying to formulate a theology of revelation which would accommodate without nullifying the apocalyptic perspective of the New Testament as he saw it."[22] That required a heady risk, reconciling truth with change without changing truth or denying the truth of change. In turn, the project exacted a synthesis of the interiorized and subjective Kingdom of God according to Ritschl and Harnack, and the externalized and objective eschatological Kingdom according to Weiss and Schweitzer.

Harnack had done well to develop the interior life's moral obligation to the Kingdom; but that must be the condition, not the essence, of eschatology. Harnack's concept of spiritual change as the deepening of the present life is inadequate. It must rather be "a development and transformation such as that which changes the grub into the moth," an idea Tyrrell got from Fichte.[23] In our day the diction may sound of Teilhard. In Tyrrell's time, and to his annoyance, Dean Inge compared it to the pragmatism of William James, whose lack of metaphysics von Hügel regretted. The lament was not extravagant, for in this

---

[21]Adolf Harnack, *What is Christianity?* (London: 1901), p. 267.

[22]Gabriel Daly, *Transcendence and Immanence*, op. cit., p. 141.

[23]In "The Month" Vol. 101 (February 1903), p. 136. Cf. Johann Gottlieb Fichte, *The Vocation of Man* (Indianapolis: 1956), pp. 83-154.

system the will is the creator and discerner of reality; abstract science does not attain to truth; religious truth is purely practical; and theology is too abstract to assist human response to revelation. The language has the swagger befitting a great gamble, and the desperation befitting a great gambler. Consider the enthusiasm for Fichte:

> The future Kingdom, given us in apocalyptic clothing, is, I suspect the natural *development*, not merely extension, continuation, deepening, of that inner kingdom of love which Christ describes in its own terms. His emphasis is on the life of love (as opposed to legalism) as being the true preparation for the future development of the spirit into something over-human in an over-natural environment. The *nature* of that development and of the pure will-world or society of spirits — all that he leaves *mysterious*; paints in terms of current eschatological fancies; but as to the *via* he is clear and decisive.[24]

The Refinement of Modernism

At this stage Tyrrell's language is no more ambiguous than his purpose. He must go with the progressive tide, uncertain of anything about it save that it is going somewhere. And that was enough to make it healthy. Still-water should not be drunk. The sign of stagnancy for the Modernist was the centrality of ontology in theological definitions, connoting an objectivity of truth for truth's sake which was the antithesis of the modern complex which identified truth with change for the sake of change. Even the developmental guide of St. Vincent of Lerins was inadequate to the swirling new progress. Indeed, it risks being a circular argument: "quod ubique, quod semper, quod, ab omnibus creditum est." This allowed for no notion of development other

---

[24]In David G. Schultenover, *George Tyrrell: In Search of Catholicism* (Shepherdstown: 1981), p. 268.

than the "explication" physiology of a medieval view which saw the final result nascent in the first instance of perception.[25] Something other was needed as a critical system for the Modernism which Tyrrell at last was beginning to define: "A philosophy of Catholic experience or practice, distinguishing what is life-giving and permanent in beliefs and usages — what saints have lived on. It tries to reconcile this with modern knowledge. It seeks a fuller and deeper, not a thinner and shallower explanation."[26] So much for Harnack's quest of a simpler Gospel. But they agreed on this: modern knowledge challenges faith in mystery.

Why this challenge should be so is another matter, and the Modernists may be faulted for a naïve social philosophy. That mystery and scientific progress are antithetical was assumed to be a positive and sound thesis. At the start of the twentieth century the assumption was more plausible than now. But Tyrrell did realize that the modern age was the first to entertain, and widely practice, existence without belief in God or transcendental purpose, as though such were normal. The Modernist passion for accepting the challenge is as instinctive as its uncritical acceptance of its premise. Tyrrell opposes Inge on other things but grants his matter-of-factness on one point: "There is still enough superstition left to win a certain vogue for miraculous cures at Lourdes . . . But that kind of religion is doomed, and will not survive three generations of sound secular education given equally to both sexes." With confidence, Voltaire had waited upon the next generation, too; and so does the remnant Liberal theologian now. The generation which Inge craned his neck to view has arrived, and its educated people of both sexes are flying to Lourdes in jets. The argument from inevitability works neither for nor against supernaturalism. Inge's other assertion demands more consideration: "The crisis of faith cannot be dealt with by

---

[25]George Tyrrell, *The Church and the Future*, privately printed 1903 (London: 1910), pp. 28-29. In Schultenover, op. cit., p. 290.

[26]*Letters*, p. 300.

establishing a *modus vivendi* between scepticism and superstition. That is all that modernism offers us; and it will not do."[27]

What it should offer, according to Tyrrell, is "a synthesis between the essentials of Christianity and the assured results of criticism."[28] And as elsewhere he hopes for a synthesis between the essential truth of his religion and the essential truth of modernity."[29] This essential truth evidently is the conclusion of its criticism, and that can only be a certain reductionism. Essentialism, then, is as much a motivation as it was for Harnack. But by way of synthesis, simplicity would be but one element; the simplicity of interior assent complements the complex ecclesiological economy by which that doctrine develops. Catholic Modernism would "purify the Catholic idea more and more from all foreign admixture and build it up member by member, nearing, yet never reaching, a perfect disclosure of its organic unity, its simplicity in complexity, its transcendent beauty."[30]

Each of the Modernist writers worked out a different expression and, among them, Tyrrell is by no means distinguished by consistency. However, in his program can be traced the outline of five concerns.[31] Catholicism has an exclusive and dogmatic character which is necessary but which should not obstruct dialogue with all things necessary to the life of a culture; Tyrrell is not Latitudinarian. Catholicism is not the moral conscience of the state though it is the organ for sanctifying its own members to further the commonweal; Tyrrell is not Erastian, even when he conveniently glances away from the French Constitutional Church's subservience to the state at one point

---

[27]Inge, *Outspoken Essays*, op. cit., pp. 169-170.

[28]*Christianity at the Cross-Roads*, p. 19.

[29]Ibid., p. 26.

[30]George Tyrrell, *Hard Sayings: A Selection of Meditations and Studies* (London: 1898), p. xvii.

[31]Cf. Schultenover, op. cit., pp. 70ff.

when he extols its ecclesiology.[32]   The deposit of faith, which consists of Scripture and tradition dogmatically defined in propositions, does not change, though its interpretation by doctrine does. The Church must constantly retranslate dogmatic propositions idiomatically, apart from scholastic philosophy and Latin diction. Catholicism is an external religion; that is, it is an experiential appeal of sacraments, hierarchical authority, dogma and sacred texts for the obedience of souls; intellectual assent to doctrine is accidental and not essential.

The various ways the Modernists altered and amplified this scheme easily escapes comprehensive analysis. Lack of anything more schematic would understandably seem cynical, or even subterfuge, to the scholastic eye. Pius X complained in *Pascendi*: "It is one of the cleverest devices of the Modernists (as they are commonly and rightly called) to present their doctrines without order and systematic arrangement, in a scattered and disjointed manner, so as to make it appear as if their minds were in doubt or hesitation, whereas in reality they are quite fixed and steadfast." And with the perception of a form critic, belying the incapacity which critics imputed to his censoriousness, he observes in the modernist a manifold personality: "he is a philosopher, a believer, a theologian, an historian, a critic, an apologist, a reformer, these roles must be clearly distinguished one from another . . ."

Tyrrell could have served his movement better had he distinguished so clearly himself.   Of such distinctions, the ambitious Modernists seemed quite incapable; in the proportion to which they were not Catholic in doctrine, they were catholic in their taste for an eclectic assortment of disciplines enlisted to serve their ends. The fatal issue was a reduction of Catholicism to dilettantism. Critical reservations about sceptical pragmatism and immanent idealism were swept away in the Modernists' enthusiasm for adapting Catholic teaching to the latest higher

---

[32]*Letters* (December 7, 1906), p. 103.

criticism and developments in physical science.[33]   If their expressions varied, their bedazzlement by such philosophical conceits molded the Modernists into a movement and a fraternity. While Sabatier thought the depiction of Modernism by *Pascendi* not a portrait but a caricature, A. L. Lilley, an Anglican friend of the movement, admitted that "since they had a common inspiration and a common purpose, it was neither unnatural nor unfair that the authority which condemned them should unite them in a common designation and in a common cause."[34]

Toward a Universal Religion

When Tyrrell sounds at times on the verge of drowning in his own syntax, one remembers that the Baron von Hügel was wont to urge him into depths he himself preferred to scout from the shore. Voices like Maisie Ward and Bernard Reardon distanced von Hügel theologically from the energetic Modernists in his doubts about immanentism and pragmatism, but in a book published the same year as Reardon's, Alec Vidler made a strong case for calling him the "chief engineer" of the whole Modernist venture.[35] He was more than its "friend." He was a man of "perduring heterodoxy" whose persuasive powers and critical faculties, superior to those of Blondel, at last convinced even William Sanday to make a more liberal reading of the Fourth Gospel, and without whom, as Maude Petre contended, Tyrrell would have been a spiritual and moral "pioneer," but would not accurately have been called a Modernist. D. A. Binchey offers a

---

[33]Cf. Letter of Edward Watkin (August 26, 1937) in Maisie Ward, *Insurrection versus Resurrection* (New York: 1937), p. 500.

[34]In Roger Aubert, *The Christian Centuries* Vol. II: *The Church in a Secularised Society* (London: 1978), p. 198, fn. 17.

[35]*Vidler,* pp. 109-126. Cf. Bernard Reardon, *Roman Catholic Modernism* (London: 1970), p. 50.

picturesque analogy: "...to deny that von Hügel was a
Modernist would be rather like refusing to include Pusey among
the leaders of the Oxford Movement because he did not follow
Newman over to Rome."[36] Receiving an honorary LL.D. from
the University of St. Andrew's in 1906, however, the Baron's
impression of discipline almost reached Curial heights as he
scorned "the denial of any and all necessary, abiding connections
between factual happenings in general and religious faith."[37]

Not always did those connections obtain in himself, as
Maisie Ward allows in a verbal arabesque of politeness and an
unintentional indictment of a mind which claims an affinity of
reality and religion: "...anyone who spends the greater part of

---

[36]"The Modernist Movement," in *The Cambridge Journal* (January
1948), p. 225.

[37]Cf. James T. Burtchaell, *Catholic Theories of Biblical Inspiration
since 1816* (Cambridge: 1969), p. 203. The Baron thought in German
even when he wrote in English, and the prolix result, not docile to
parsing, can be confusing if not completely ambiguous. Writing many
years later, he defines two kinds of "Modernism": the first being the
ongoing task of interpreting the permanent truths of the Faith
according to the best contemporary philosophy and scholarship and
science. The second kind, which he vainly thought was "over and
done," consisted in "the series or groups of specific attempts, good,
bad, indifferent, or variously mixed, that were made towards similar
expressions or interpretations, ... ending with the death of Fr. T. and
with Loisy's alienation from the positive content that had been fought
for ..." etc. (q.v.) Sensitive to the suspicion that something of Humpty
Dumpty was in his definitions, he denied that his fogginess was self-
justifying camouflage. He thinks the Church's censures were "violent
and unjust," yet however: "...it is not cowardice or policy, it is in
simplest sincerity, that I have come to see, more clearly than I used to
do, how much of serious unsatisfactoriness and of danger there was
especially in many of the philosophical (strongly subjectivist) theories
really held which *Pascendi* lumped together.... The actual fact of a
very real, though certainly not unlimited submission, and the duty of
such submission — I care much should not be left uncertain on
occasion, in my own case." (To Miss Maude Petre, March 13, 1918), in
Baron Friedrich von Hügel, *Selected Letters 1896-1924*, ed. Barnard
Holland (London: 1928), pp. 248f.

his time in meditation on ultimate issues is likely to suffer from a certain want of focus when he is forced to establish relations with the world of every day."[38] Tyrrell wrote of a visit from von Hügel: "Wonderful man! Nothing is true; but the sum total of nothings is sublime. Christ was not merely ignorant but a tête brulé (sic)..." Taking into account that Tyrrell was in the last throes of his fatal disease, the impression is not to be discounted. Such at least was the impact on a delicate psychology, and in light of it, the Pope's lack of confidence in what the Modernist's were really about is reasonable. Von Hügel eventually asked that his name be deleted by the publisher from the Introduction to the final work of Tyrrell to whom he had been a kind of Erasmus; it was an instance of shrunken nobility in the minor nobleman.

Tyrrell might have remained incoherently enamored of both Harnack and Schweitzer, had not the Baron introduced him to the writings of Loisy. The Liberal mixture of rationalism and sentimentalism went under Loisy's scalpel in *L'Évangile et l'Église*, an apology for cynicism so subtle that Pius X as Cardinal Sarto was greatly pleased with all but a few "obscure" passages. Tyrrell probed the book more deeply and resolved to amplify its "scientific" but latent development theory. Christianity would not be reduced to the Liberal indignity of a mere ethic subjectively decided. As Weiss and Schweitzer had spared few pains to insist, the Gospel is a compendium of ideas indicative of the Kingdom of God inaugurated, though not fulfilled, by Jesus in his day. The Church prepares the world for the Kingdom and quickens mankind's hope. The Church is not the Kingdom, nor is the Gospel; but they are partners bringing humanity into it. And as this is a progressive relationship, adaptations such as Hellenization over the years attest to its vitality; they can only be corrupting agents in Harnack's picture of an original fixed Christianity, a pierce of porcelain not to be broken. But Harnack

---

[38]Maisie Ward, op. cit., p. 497. *Letters* (August 14, 1908). Cf. Cuthbert Butler, *Religions of Authority and the Religion of the Spirit* (London: 1930), pp. 179ff.

was no more mistaken, concluded Tyrrell, than were the scholastics who thought in terms of an original deposit of systematic dogmas entrusted to an apostolic order whose duty was to preserve it by autonomous authority from heterodox erosion.

Loisy's injurious influence on Tyrrell centered in his departure from Newman's conformity of development theory to orthodox dogma, and particularly in his teaching that the content of dogma is mutable because of its analogical nature. "Truth alone is unchangeable, but not its image in our minds."[39] Platonism so teased became Platonism tortured:

> The conceptions that the Church presents as revealed dogma are not truths fallen from heaven and preserved by religious tradition in the precise form in which they first appeared. The historian sees in them the interpretation of religious facts, acquired by a laborious effort of theological thought. Though the dogma may be divine in origin and substance, they are human in structure and composition. It is inconceivable that their future should not correspond to their past.[40]

Through Loisy came Tyrrell's effective contact with a refinement of Sabatier's phases of subjective epistemology in religion and morals. There are three moments in religious experience: the interior revelation of God which tends to formal religion through subjective human piety; interpretations of revelation which pass through formulas into creeds; and the third which is Christianity itself, not the climactic moment but the best expression of religious sentiment in the contemporary milieu, destined to evolve into a more perfect form of religion, and one far more suitable to the analogical character of revealed truth. But all this must be read bearing in mind that Loisy had already denied the supernatural content of Christianity; that which is supernatural is the consistent inclination of faith *ver le mieux*.

---

[39]Loisy, *L'Évangile et l'Église*, op. cit., p. 217.
[40]Ibid., pp. 210-211.

Unless Loisy is read from that assumption, and he did not confess it in his coy introduction to *L'Évangile*, the book could, as it did, strike the most traditional readers as positively sound. For to say dogmas do not drop fully formed from heaven is stating the obvious, unless the writer says it as a literal cipher meaning that dogmas are not heavenly. In this prescription, the Bible is only an historical account of religion's sources; it can no longer be looked upon by rightly guided faith as a rule or source of belief. To say otherwise, even to attribute divine authority to a limited definition of the Gospel as did the Liberals, is infantile anthropomorphism.[41] In 1912, Loisy would admit to Harnack that he was heterodox as far back as 1885. One cannot even be sure whether his own responses to Harnack in the form of *L'Évangile* was an attempt to justify his reduced Catholicism, or simply a charade announcing to the subtle that the reduction of a zero is always zero. In 1907 he would unambiguously represent himself as an atheist.

Evidently, Tyrrell was unaware of Loisy's double profile. In an 1899 issue of "The Month" he had published a complement to Loisy's use of Sabatier. Shortly afterward, another article on "The Revelation of Theology to Devotion" marked what he called a "turning point" in his life, for in it he denied the legitimacy of revealed theology.[42] In 1906 he would confess to Wilfrid Ward what he had already defined in print and would reproduce in book form:

> I believe in revelation as a man of faith, I believe in theology as a man of reason; I believe each helps and depends on the other, but that the bastard progeny of their mixture is not *a priori* only, but historically the enemy of both, the parent of unbelief and ignorance. So, too, the authority of Church government is lawful and necessary, it is ministerial to spiritual authority — but it is not "divine" in the same direct

---

[41]Loisy, *Autour d'un petit livre* (Paris: 1903), pp. 50-51.
[42]"The Month," Vol. 94.

sense any more than theological thought is divine in the same sense as revelation.[43]

So much then for *lex orandi lex credendi*; the heart and mind are not in dialogue but in tension. Primitive revelation is "perhaps more directly a *lex orandi* than a *lex credendi*." Any latent ambiguity yields to contradiction, for in the same text he defends and denies the unique claims of apostolic authority in the primitive texts for determining the authentic development of tradition.[44]

What to him formerly had seemed Newman's genius in the *Essay of the Development of Doctrine* now was a gift for fantasy, imagining a doctrine that might change and remain the same. In 1902, he writes a piece on "The Limitations of Newman" and then tells Ward: "The importance of Newman's line is that it prepares a philosophical and rationalistic theory of Church authority which will (or may possibly) stand when the 'miraculous' theory shall have gone the way of all fond illusions."[45] The fissure with the old Cardinal has been compared to Schoenberg's break from the tonal system of Wagner; it certainly was no more harmonic.[46] Both had understood that Protestant criticism was fatally flawed by imagining the Word revealed in Scripture as an entity apart from the Church and to which the Church must conform; rather, the Word lives in the Church and the Church is its authenticating criterion.[47] Newman's flaw, in the eye of his young critic, was his undue scholastic acceptance of revelation as propositional. Newman ignored the role of experience in Scripture, disallowing the function of human response to its primary prophetic vision. It was precisely on this point, curious to say, that Kähler's version of

---

[43]*Letters* (to Wilfrid Ward, April 8, 1906), p. 101.

[44]*Scylla and Charybdis*, pp. 9-10. Cf. Burtchaell, op. cit., p. 208.

[45]*Letters* (August 1, 1903), p. 76.

[46]Gabriel Daly, *Transcendence and Immanence*, op. cit., pp. 155-156.

[47]Cf. Joseph Ratzinger, *Das Neue Volk Gottes* (Dusseldorf: 1969), p. 106.

credo in ecclesiam in his Protestant context is more consistent than Tyrrell's; while Kähler lapsed into pure supra-historicity and rejected the propositional use of Scripture, he did reject the commanding consequences of the faith of the whole Church. Kähler chooses to deconstruct the way Christ is preached; Tyrrell deconstructs how Christ is Christ. The sources of this Modernist line did indeed have its nurture in the supra-historical critique and its blemished inheritance of the Kantian configuration of reason and religion; but as Modernism argued from Catholic sources, it took the Church more seriously as the equivalent of history.

Given the organic nature of tradition and the structures of tradition, the Modernist's antipathy to authority inevitably became antipathy to what the authority preaches. That really was at the bottom of its rejection of scholasticism, and it became a rupture within traditional belief far more portentous than what Kähler had attempted when he distanced himself from the propositional use of Scripture according to orthodox Protestantism. Tyrrell's absurd claim that Newman neglected experience, when in fact the absorbing account of experience in the process of assent made Newman suspect to the myopic eyes of some contemporary Catholics who understood neither Augustine nor Aquinas, exposes his subjectivist prejudice. This is what made him Schoenberg to Newman's Wagner, or better to Newman's Beethoven. Schoenberg's new creation was atonalism and the various manifestations of Modernism introduced something quite as jarring. Whether this was a splendid new symphony for modern man or a mocking cacophony surrendering to modern man's frustration, depends on whether it is heard in a peaceful Edwardian breeze tossling the hair of white-clad youths on a sunny cricket lawn, or at the end of the same century with wind rattling through unfriendly fields of carnage and chrome halls of harsh commerce.

Newman had set tests for development of doctrine: preservation of type, continuity of principles, power of assimilation, logical sequence, anticipation of results, conservation of the old, chronic vigor. All these were instruments of right decision, he said, but the true guarantee is authentication by the Church in response to an issue. Newman could not have objected to some sensible lines of Arthur Kenny:

> The multiplication of definitions does not, merely in itself, raise any problems concerning the immutability of faith. The avowed purpose of the majority of conciliar and papal definitions has not been to make change or addition to the beliefs of orthodox Christians, but rather to provide a legal instrument for the reform of expulsion of heretics alleged to have denied an article of faith hitherto an unquestioned part of the Christian patrimony of belief. It has never, so far as I know, been officially defined that Jesus was a man — a male, and not a woman — because there has never been a feminist heresy to deny this truth. But if a group began to propound such a heresy, and it was condemned under anathema, the Pope could scarcely be reproached with altering, or adding, to the faith handed down from the Apostles.[48]

We are now watching this at work in a lively way. Since Kenny wrote in 1964, the Church has faced the very heresy to which he alludes, whether one calls it surface gnosticism or radical feminism; and she has indicated that the facts of sexuality extend beyond juridicism to a basic ontology of the priestly order in creation. But for us the issue at hand is the way in which Tyrrell's embrace of subjectivism led him farther from the Catholicism he had sought to defend against ultramontanism and rationalism alike, and into a gnostic paradigm for the totality of salvation history. He widened his new embrace in yet another book in 1907, *Through Scylla and Charybdis: or the Old Theology and the New*. The metaphor had a long use by theologians. Tyrrell may not have remembered how the Puritans had remonstrated in 1651: "Our former Warning ... hes stiered a

---

[48]Arthur Kenny, *Reason and Religion: Essays in Philosophical Theology* (Oxford: 1987), pp. 23-24.

steadie course between the Shylla of Malignants and Charibdis of Sectaries." More likely would he have recalled the irony of the *Apologia* where Newman quotes an article of 1839; there he spoke of contemporary Liberals who would guide the Church through the channel of no-meaning, between the Scylla and Charybdis of Aye and No." Had Newman been raised up to haunt Tyrrell for toying so with his theory of development he could have done no better than the examination of conscience he left:

> In the present day, mistiness is the method of wisdom. A man who can set down half-a-dozen general propositions, which escape from destroying one another only by being diluted into truisms, who can hold the balance between opposites so skillfully as to do without fulcrum or beam, who never enunciates a truth without guarding himself against being supposed to exclude the contradictory, — who holds that Scripture is the only authority, yet that the Church is to be deferred to, that faith only justifies, yet that it does not justify without works, that grace does not depend on the sacraments, yet is not given without them, that bishops are a divine ordinance, yet those who have them not are in the same religious condition as those who have, — this is your safe man and the hope of the Church.[49]

Understandably, the spirit of Newman became an unsettling ghost to Tyrrell. Understandably, von Hügel thought Newman holy but depressing. Understandably, the self-obsessed Bremond wrote to the exiled Loisy: "What touches me most, in your case as in Tyrrell's, is to see the ego does not engross your autobiographies, as it does engross, deplorably in my view, Newman's *Apologia*."[50]

The extremes against which Tyrrell had argued, the rocks between which he would pass, suddenly loomed larger. They became deism and pantheism in "Il Rinnovemento" (April 1907),

---

[49]John Henry Newman, *Apologia pro Vita Sua* (London: 1890, orig. 1891), p. 103.

[50]Bremond to Loisy (June 15, 1913), in *Vidler*, p. 31.

the short-lived Modernist journal in Milan; and the "deists" included the scholastics with their "false" transcendence. It is no more strained than his calling ultramontanism "a species of Protestantism."[51] Invectives of this order belong to his last days, the dark time of name-calling. Anyone similarly tormented could have called him close to a pantheist, or monist, for the writing into which he was declining: "It is He who, in conjunction with (the soul) and with His whole creation — as it were, one Self, one Subject, — desires and seeks the universal good whereby all creatures enter into the eternal joy of their Lord . . ."[52]

His professed rejection of propositions notwithstanding, the young lightning rod of Modernism envisioned a body of doctrine so developed that it would become a new Catholicism different from the form riveted to Rome. Its character would be the compatibility between mystical desire for God and the modern expectation of what God must be. The Alpha revealed would become the *a priori* intuited, and the sacred tradition guiding it would be none other than the sacredness of life itself. Theology as such becomes theosophy. "There are not only Modernist Roman Catholics, but Modernist Anglicans and nonconformists — nay Modernist Jews and Musulmans."[53] As a forward and inclusive direction, this was a challenge to Harnack's backward quest which devolved upon a Christ shaved of all the barbaric embellishments of religion, tribe and caste. When Harnack barbered the Messiah he found a simple and highly moral German professor with Lutheran sympathies. Tyrrell would rather let the Messiah run wild through the many different temples and factories of civilization proclaiming that to be Catholic and to be Modern is the same purpose of creation, and the function of the Messiah is not to baptize modern people but to baptize their modernity. Redemption is the transformation of

---

[51]*Letters* (January 13, 1909), p. 119.

[52]George Tyrrell, *Oil and Wine*, privately printed 1902 (London: 1907), p. 221.

[53]*Christianity at the Cross-Roads*, p. 29.

an adjective into a noun, the making of *modern* into a quasi-mystical *Modernism*. And thus Catholicism ceases to be a fact and becomes a function: Catholicism is "Modernism *par excellence*, the first to bear the name and pass it on to analogous movements . . ." It takes its primacy among religions because in it "the opposition between old and new is more precise and acute . . . than in any other."[54] The Modernist would hardly get so much attention were he not claiming to be a Catholic.

Having rejected the material humanism of Liberal Protestantism, a professor in the Union Theological Seminary in New York City, an excommunicated Presbyterian who had become an Episcopalian, offered to join Tyrrell's crusade as a self-styled Protestant Modernist. Charles Augustus Briggs (1841-1913) held, "The Modernists, who have been smitten by the Roman Catholic and Protestant Churches alike, are for the most part, not radicals but conservatives . . ." They only seek new ways of saying old things. They do not intend to destroy the mystical element in religion as did the Liberal Protestants. The claim was as essentialist as Harnack, though where the essence for Harnack was morality, the essence for the Modernist was mysticism. Briggs's higher criticism was not so radical as Harnack's, though what he means by modern and liberal and progressive is unrefined, and his impression of the Modernists is romantic. In the years of "Pascendi" he writes:

> The Modernists in the Roman Catholic Church are modernists in that they use modern methods in theology. They do not differ from Mediaevalists in the doctrines of the Church but only in the form and mode of stating them . . . This is precisely the same conflict that has been in progress all over the Protestant world between Protestant scholastics and progressive Protestants: between those who insist that the scholastic formulas of the seventeenth century should be binding, as well as the doctrines contained in them . . . it is no longer a battle between Protestants and Roman

---

[54]Ibid., pp. 28-29.

> Catholics ... Modernists, Protestants and Catholics alike,
> are characterized by these same things."[55]

Enthusiasm of such American proportions could have made Tyrrell skittish and would have sent a nervous von Hügel scurrying back to his study to write more soberly about the mystical element in religion. But Briggs presciently described the realignment of theological positions as it has come to pass at the end of the twentieth century. "Scholastics" and "progressivists" do indeed cut across the various denominational stratifications. And the elephantine scale of the Modernist confidence in a synthesis of religious moods has found recent issue, too. The contemporary element in Catholicism which distinguishes between Vatican II, and the "Spirit of Vatican II" which it hopes will issue in an inchoate mysticism of bourgeois intuitions, has a forerunner in Tyrrell's vision of a Utopian Church as home for all Idealists. "I do not think we have yet the data to answer the problem of the religion of the Future; but I feel more and more that it will be a more thoroughly Christian and more thoroughly 'Catholic' form of religion than yet realized."[56] The "Future" is capitalized by the Modernist as the most romantic reactionary would not dare do of the "past."

As Kant had discerned divine being in reason distinct from man, as a Liberal Protestantism has discerned it ultimately in man himself, Tyrrell dimly outlined it in a "religion of humanity" made of a "deep reality and fuller spiritual substance than the various forms of Positivism can offer ..."[57] Yet what could sound more like Comte's grand phrases than Tyrrell's talk, in this same passage, of a "God-idea of a whole people?" He tended to sacramentalize the categorical imperative when he described

---

[55]Charles Augustus Briggs, *Church Unity*, 1909 in William J. Hynes, "A Hidden Nexus between Catholic and Protestant Modernism," *The Downside Review* (July 1987), Vol. 105, No. 360.

[56]Letter to R. Abbott (August 1904), in *Autobiography and Life*, op. cit., Vol. II, p. 407.

[57]*Letters* (1908), p. 32.

religion as the zeal which animates morality, giving duty a sacred character. Nor was he less than forthright about Idealism as the constituent philosophy of modernism. "Faith in the Kantian sense — that is, a reasonable submission to quasi-instinctive belief and sentiments, philosophically unjustified — is as necessary for science as for ethics or theology."[58] The zeal was genuine, but only as bravado; and bravado does not lend itself to the precision which makes sense of classical theology as a science. By an apparent incomprehension of reason and intelligence as they obtain in the scholastic system, for example, the Idealist cannot account for St. Bernard's fraternity of mysticism and scholasticism except to say fantastically, "they could not more blend than oil and water"; Tyrrell insists that scholastic epistemology (*nihil in intellectu nisi quod prius in sensu*) was purely external and non-mystical intellectualism.[59] Churches are emptied not by ignorance but by intellectual tyranny: "It is because St. Thomas Aquinas is imposed on us, rather than because Kant is ignored."[60]

If Tyrrell remains any more of a supernaturalist than Loisy, it is in the vestigial sense that Feuerbach applied to Kant and Fichte and Hegel. It is true that he does not claim to refute grace; but his is an agnosticism in which natural religion has no part in leading to supernatural evidences. At times he engages his own dialectic between dogma inaccessible to reason according to Kant, and a mysticism accessible to unaided reason according to Hegel. "Il Rinnovamente" publicly declared its intention to speak for "all aspects of modern, subjectivist, post-Kantian philosophy in so far as these could be accommodated to faith in the transcendence of a personal God and in revelation." But the rational adhesion of the mind to postulates of practical reason which marks faith for Kant is rejected by Tyrrell for a faith which

---

[58] In "The Month," Vol. 83 (May 1899), p. 27. Cf. Schultenover, op. cit., p. 194.

[59] *Letters* (October 25, 1907), pp. 53-54.

[60] Ibid. (August 29, 1907), p. 134.

is rationally inexplicable, a commitment to the Unknowable. Dogmas are debased by Kant to catechetical formulas in order to inculcate morality in the unintelligent and the young; for Tyrrell they correspond, however ephemerally, to a need of human nature. Prayer has no purpose for Kant; it becomes everything for Tyrrell. A gnostic bias still obtains; for the prayer is essentially subjective mind control, different from Christian obedience to a divine will.

Tyrrell's foundations for all this can be traced through Sabatier, whose radical subjectivism he claimed to reject, to Schleiermacher's apologetic approach to science, and Spencer's evolutionism. But finally, the complex Modernist account of dogma and sacramental symbols integrated into this *potpourri* contradicts the Modernist's immanentist antipathy to extrinsicism. It may be that the Modernists' sensitivity to their own contradiction makes them as defensive against the Liberal Protestants as they are to the scholastics. One evidence of Tyrrell's insecurity is his frequent lapse into Liberal phrases, e.g.: "To be a Christian is to believe in the teaching of Christ — not necessarily in the theological amplification of that teaching."[61]

Harnack had not outrightly repudiated the worship accorded to Christ, but it made no objective sense and was idolatrous, though not without a certain therapeutic effect. Tyrrell's aestheticism admired Loisy's justification of such worship which, given the state of Loisy's own faith, is remarkable only for explaining why he continued to offer Mass after he ceased to believe that Christ is offered in it. Thus began the Modernist school of liturgics which reduces ecclesiastical ritual to anthropologically interesting rites of passage and communalization. For Loisy, prayer "derives its value from the feeling that prompts it and determines its moral efficacy, not from the occasion that provokes it, not even from the good to which it seems directed. This efficacy of prayer is independent of its

---

[61]Ibid. (February 22, 1908), p. 55.

formal fulfillment, and is no more a matter of question for the Christian than the personal existence of God." The "worship of saints, or relics, of the Virgin, and of the Saviour himself" is justified on the ground of psychological benefit which Liberal speculations on the pure essence of Christianity are unable to produce: "Herr Harnack recognizes that devotions paid to the sacred Heart, the holy Virgin, and others, have become in the Catholic Church a source of blessing and a means of reaching the good."[62] And this Loisy commends even though at that time Harnack probably took the moral influence of Christ more seriously and less anthropologically than he.

The Final Frustration

The more that Modernists used the language of traditional piety so deftly, and with such compelling romance, the more the reader may misjudge their eclectic Idealism. And then it would be possible for prejudice to gloss over faults and to make interpretive blunders about their Christology and sacramental theology, let alone their ecclesiology. Consequently, there have been frail apologies for Tyrrell's tragic figure, like this humbug: "(Tyrrell) hoped that there was room in Catholicism for freedom as well as the general teachings of the Church. His writings constantly point toward the wider dimensions of Catholicism."[63] The sea without shores then becomes shores without a sea. Another speaks of Tyrrell's "sense of loss, a loss that centered in the deprivation of his priestly privileges and a loss that would pain him till his death."[64] It is an expression found in all sympathetic biographies, a flagrancy of bathos in the name of criticism. But in none of these, and astonishingly not in

---

[62]Loisy, *L'Évangile et l'Église*, op. cit., pp. 270f.

[63]Ellen Leonard, C.S.J., *George Tyrrell and the Catholic Tradition* (London: 1982), pp. 35-36.

[64]Schultenover, op. cit., p. 327.

Schultenover's detailed journal of the correspondence at the time of Tyrrell's suspension *a divinis*, is there any mention of his letter to Wilfrid Ward which tells nonchalantly of the possibility of suspension from the clerical state: "For my own devotion I always preferred hearing to saying Mass, and to occupy the layman's part of the Church, being too democratic even to enjoy the 'superiority' of sacerdotal dignity. A Roman collar always chokes me, though I wear it still for propriety's sake."[65]

Catholicism, he said, "is no mere juridical bond to be snapped at the word of an angry bishop..."[66] The expression is telling; to his highstrung mind a bishop must almost by definition be angry. If a bishop had a word to say, it would not be placid and certainly not holy. The word of a bishop could not be the word of a bishop apart from a dark motive. The only exception was the Modernist prelate, Mignot of Frejus who died Archbishop of Albi; and in all of the past the one model was the improbable figure of the French revolutionary schismatic Grégoire. The complex turns mendacious when he treats of Cardinal Mercier who had gone out of his way to befriend him: "...boldly throw open the doors and windows of your great mediaeval cathedral, and let the light of a new day strike into its darkest corners and the fresh wind of Heaven blow through its mouldy cloisters."[67] It is a peroration worthy of Harnack. Tyrrell longed for that day when the "lay mind will quietly impose a democratic interpretation on the existing ecclesiastical hierarchy through its growing inability to understand authority in any other way than as deriving from the whole community."[68] *The London Quarterly Review*, with the abiding affinity of the media for anyone taking up a David's sling against the papal Goliath, would soon mourn the "eloquent, poignant tones pleading that the best

---

[65]*Letters* (April 8, 1906), p. 102.

[66]*Scylla and Charybdis*, p. 81.

[67]George Tyrrell, *Mediaevalism: A Reply to Cardinal Mercier* (London: 1908), pp. 35-36.

[68]*Letters* (December 7, 1906), p. 103.

in Roman Catholicism should be liberated from Pope and Curia and Congregations of Cardinals . . ."[69]

The anguish of rejection, which cannot serve the office of mortification in febrile minds and only corrodes the proud, takes its toll on the quality of consistency and the grace of charity. The voice had been poignant, if uncomprehending, about the souls of the saints: "Is not their very reverence, humility, and obedience the reason of their mental passivity and incapacity for criticism?" The author could not be faulted for mental passivity and incapacity for criticism. Thus, only five years later: "The Curé d'Ars was as ignorant and stupid as Pius X."[70] This was from the man whose motive was the dignity of the common man and the simplicity of holiness. A truth which comes at the price of one's own life has exacted a fair exchange; but a truth which costs charity is not a truth of religion. Now humor can be an outward side of charity which is never assured by its neglect; the humor of the Modernists is conspicuous by its absence, but no more than the gift of discernment. With what long faces do these men proclaim the joy of a new world from which the cloak of Scholastic darkness has been pulled away; and with what melancholy do they berate the darkness of the sunny clerks of Rome. In two places, a sympathetic biographer tells us that Pius X announced in Consistory on April 17, 1907 that he was "after blood."[71] The Pontiff simply was using a protocol formula of address, obvious even in translation, invoking the Cardinals' vow to defend the Pope with their lives. If Pope Pius raised the possibility of exacting blood, it was the blood of his Curia.

In "Lamentabile," n. 57, the Pope upheld the validity of progress in the natural theological sciences. He had told Loisy's bishop: "Treat him kindly, and if he takes one step towards you,

---

[69]Ibid. (January 1910), p. 136.
[70]Ibid. (November 22, 1908); cf. ibid. (August 1, 1903), p. 76.
[71]Schultenover, op. cit., pp. 338, 340.

take two towards him."[72] But the cruelest thing "Lamentabile" could have done, though it was cruel as justice, was to condemn last of all the proposition: "Modern Catholicism can be reconciled with true science only if it is transformed into a non-dogmatic Christianity; that is to say, into a broad and liberal Protestantism." Critics complained that this totally misjudged Modernism's motive. But is it possible that St. Pius X saw in terms of final ends what the Modernists were blinded by their method from seeing themselves? Liberal Protestantism wanted a Gospel without a Church; Catholic Modernism wanted a Church without a Gospel. Tyrrell claimed that Catholicism brought him closer to Christianity.[73] If the unity of Christian truth does not subsist in the Catholic Church which has been endowed with all divinely revealed truth and with all means of grace as the Second Vatican Council taught, then it is an essence as ineffable as the moralizings of the Liberals.[74]

There are those who have said that Tyrrell refused to isolate one expression of Catholicism as exclusively synonymous with the totality of Catholic tradition. But what, then, is that tradition? If it is experiential, how could one object to Pius IX's fabled exclamation: "La tradizione sono io?" Inescapably, the faith of the Modernists had separated from the faith of the Catholic Church; it was unmitigated clericalism despite all its protestations of laicism; it was ecclesiasticism as a mental habit and not a habit of grace, and to that extent it was a vice. The ex-priest Gregory Baum put his own construction on the Second Vatican Council and regretted in Tyrrell "a cultural Toryism that made him accept hierarchy in Church and society as part of the world God had created."[75] In so speaking, he takes Modernism

---

[72]J. Derek Holmes, *The Triumph of the Holy See* (London: 1978), p. 265.

[73]*Autobiography and Life*, op. cit., pp. 111-112.

[74]Con. Vat. II, "Unitatis Redingratio," n. 4.

[75]Introduction to Ellen Leonard, *George Tyrrell and the Catholic Tradition*, op. cit., p. xvii.

to lengths the Modernists did not anticipate, though Pius X did. One Protestant wrote to von Hügel: "Though I call myself a non-Catholic I ought to explain that if Father Tyrrell's conception of Church authority had been tolerated by the authorities, I should now be a Roman Catholic..."[76] But what would that Church be? Professor Macquarrie says of Hans Küng's *On Being a Christian* and *Does God Exist?*: "There can be little doubt that these two books have brought many people into the Catholic Church and have kept within it many others who might have left. It is, therefore, regrettable that the ecclesiastical authorities have deprived Küng of his status as a Catholic teacher on the grounds of his alleged unorthodoxy on such questions as papal infallibility."[77] But what did those many think they were joining, and what do those many others now think they have retained?

Here glistens a bare "Essence of Catholicism" as ephemeral as the "Essence of Christianity" once preached in the University of Berlin. The search for an essence becomes heretical when essentialism functions as a philosophical substitute for purity of doctrine; the essentialist is a menace because he despises purity as only a puritan can. The Revised Code of Canon Law (751) defines heresy in favor of the unity of belief: "Heresy is the obstinate post-baptismal denial of some truth which must be believed with divine and catholic faith, or it is likewise an obstinate doubt concerning the same." And when one denies the point being made in declaring a theologian heretical, one slides into the uncritical imputation of prophecy to everyone so declared. It is true that Aquinas was indicted and Teresa was summoned to the dock, but they did not forswear the unity of faith to press their own points, and within the context of that unity they were declared right when it was understood that they were not wrong. But Arius was not right because he was called wrong, nor was Huss or Zwingli; and the stamp of their heresy

---

[76]Letter to von Hügel (August 1, 1909), in *Vidler*, p. 171.
[77]John Macquarrie, *Twentieth Century Religious Thought*, 3rd ed. (London: 1981), p. 404.

was the claim to absorb the unity of faith into themselves. Thomism is a way of being a Catholic, when Zwinglianism is a way of being another Zwingli. A problem in treating Modernism today is that it does not commonly separate from the Church, though it claims that the Church is separating itself from itself. So long, however, as Modernism imagines becoming greater than Catholicism, it makes itself less than Catholicism and orders itself into that disorder of belief which, doubting the unity of faith, does in fact synthesize error. That is the grave mistake of the essentialist, and by his method essence becomes essentialism, purity become puritanism, and truth united becomes synthesis. Sometimes it is called the "pastoral approach" when it is an Hegelian wolf in sheep's clothing.

From Idealist cloth George Tyrrell tried to tailor an ecclesiasticism capable of maintaining the historical continuity of Catholic experience in a subjective system of belief. As the inevitable outcome of disoriented thought which had meandered through many different minds in the aftershock of Kantianism, it became a theosophy and its theologians became cultural anthropologists. Artificiality of invention, an attempt to seam together from synthetic material a seamless and aboriginal garment, had to expect the censure of legitimate authority. Authority obliged to reality by its very obligation contradicts the assumptions of Idealism. Having dis-existentialized the scholastic commitment to the knowledge of sensible things, the Idealist feels free, and even feels obliged, to manipulate through abstractions instead of governing through facts. This may account for the Modernists' inadequacy with people; motivated by a zeal for human well-being, they were pastoral failures, populists without people, convinced as no true scholastic could have been convinced that the immaculate essence of a truth is other than the immaculate heart of a truth.

In the early life of Tyrrell there is a commonly overlooked incident, when he tracked tar on the carpet of a woman who had annoyed him. Petulant moments can be ignored unless they become a type for a lifelong habit, and we have been considering a man and a movement whose psychological reaction to papal complaint was to track tar through the halls of the Vatican. Risking the treachery of generalization, the martyrs of the Modernist Pantheon shared at least three psychological characteristics, and in the testy circumstances of that time these began as flaws and grew into malignancies: detestation of authority for being authoritative, contempt for the intellectual capacities of superiors, and servility to trends. Modernism was nothing if it was not the form of fraternity for intellectuals whose confidence of mental superiority gave them the one platform from which they might imagine that they were looking down upon those in higher places; it boasted the elevation of thinking above knowing and, as in the experience of the modern university, the shakier the platform the louder the arrogance of those on it.

Minds more realistically attached to souls will be less ready to detect injustice in every form of subordination, and obscurantism in every miracle. Reality, certainly not reality which has lived in the real world of life and living, will not long be persuaded of a "vital immanence," not any more than it will justify the confidence of Harnack's moralizings. The Modernists were pessimistic about the present Kingdom as the Liberals were optimistic about the coming Kingdom. They made their prejudice a creedless creed, and in that they have no rational appeal against the conclusion of "Pascendi." The synthesis of all heresies is a mood and moods are not religion.

Epilogue:
A Meeting of Three Wise Men

Newman, Harnack and Barth

Pope Pius XI called Karl Barth one of the great, not Catholic, theologians of the age: a papal bouquet for which Barth would reciprocate by thanking Paul VI for the Encyclical *Humanae Vitae*. The Pope's comment was made from the same sort of cultural vantage point enjoyed by that master of Catholic theology, Karl Adam, who said Barth's commentary of Romans was a bomb falling on the playground of theologians. The same Adam approvingly cited von Hügel's "all-welcoming" spirit of Catholicism, which offered "a union of nature with grace, of art with religion, of knowledge with faith..."; he also meant a selective habit of learning from experience, incorporating what good remains when removed from its dross.[1]

St. Augustine recognized, and freely promoted, the Church's office for "taking the 'gold of the Egyptians' and handing it on to her sons and daughters." The refinement of eclectic sources can unify the positive elements in apparent incompatibilities.[2] To a certain extent the previous chapters have

---

[1]Karl Adam, *The Spirit of Catholicism* (London: 1928), p. 158. Vid. Friedrich von Hügel, *The Mystical Element in Religion* Vol. II (Cambridge: 1961), p. 118. Dom Cuthbert Butler, from the evidence of a personal friendship, was struck by von Hügel's piety: "Nor was his any sort of esoteric philosophic Catholicism: he practiced the recognized popular devotions of workaday Catholicism." *Religions of Authority and The Religion of the Spirit* (London: 1930), p. 184.

[2]*De vera religione*, VIII, 15.

tried to follow this course. But such is in the order of syntheses and not of essences. If a Pope thinks Barth qualifies for a pantheon, if not the calendar of saints and doctors, this does not mean that the Swiss Protestant's theology was true for being great; it does mean that there is a power of criticism in it which for good or ill has challenged the Liberal bourgeois confidences of some of the thinkers we have considered, and has established an analysis of reason and religion which has outlived its inventor. Barth's name crops up here only because he appeared at the end of the Liberal line and reacted against it from within the Protestant continuum stretching from the radical analysis of Kant.

By the above standard, the measure of greatness may be taken of Barth more confidently than of Harnack. It can be taken of neither as confidently as it may be of Newman, though Newman's qualification and strength is that he does not profess to be a theologian. Each had his own idea of what constitutes Christianity, not synthetically but essentially. Only Harnack deliberately tried to boil it down to what he blatantly called an essence; Barth avoided the term; and Newman preferred to speak of what it boiled up to. Only Harnack and Barth knew each other, the early Barth being an obliging disciple of the master; and Barth's human virtues contributed more to their exchanges. If, say, the three gathered in some university Common Room to think aloud about the essence of Christianity, and the drama of reason and religion in its definition, it would become a very uncommon Common Room. And Newman's voice would not have been much heard, unless Barth as translator prevailed upon his retiring nature.

They would have much to talk about to be sure, and for the talking they possibly would have lined up this way: Harnack, the man who came to symbolize the Liberal Protestant ideal of essential Christianity, spends most of the time discussing Patristics with Newman, little concealing his regret that Barth is so indifferent an historian; Barth, for whom Newman and the whole English empirical tradition were like some exotic air-breathing orchids too fragile for a real garden, is fascinated with Newman's breadth of dogmatic reference, and at once takes up the question of Anselm to the annoyance of Harnack who thinks the conversation has degenerated; and then when the very word "Christology" is uttered, Newman finds himself annoying the others. Barth does not understand why Newman will not see Christology as synonymous with Christianity, and Harnack gets slightly irritated that they take it seriously at all.

Another question arises as words become sharper, and Newman raises it. Is there really such a thing as the essence of Christianity, or can it be described in any satisfactory way? In 1871 when Harnack was twenty years old, and thirteen years before Barth came into the world, Newman dedicated to William Froude an old essay of 1841 deriding those who are "ever hunting for a fabulous primitive simplicity; we repose in Catholic fullness." His lifelong search was for that fullness more than any essence. And as the course of his life's work would resolve, the fullness would become the essence. He summarizes the "External Theory" of Milman, a counterpart to Harnack's essentialism. According to it,

> Revelation was a single, entire, solitary act, or nearly so, introducing a certain message; whereas we, who maintain the other, consider that Divine teaching has been in fact, what the analogy of nature would lead us to expect, "at sundry times and in divers manners," various, complex, progressive, and supplemental of itself. We consider the Christian doctrine, when analyzed, to appear, like the human fame, "fearfully and wonderfully made"; but they think it some one tenet or certain principles given out at one time in their fullness, without gradual accretion before Christ's coming or elucidation afterwards. They cast off all they find in Pharisee or heathen; we conceive that the Church, like Aaron's rod, devours the serpents of the magicians ... They seek what never has been found; we accept and use what even they acknowledge to be a substance. They are driven to maintain, on their part, that

the Church's doctrine was never pure; we say that it never can be corrupt. We consider that a divine promise keeps the Church Catholic from doctrinal corruption; but on what promise, or on what encouragement, they are seeking for their visionary purity does not appear.[3]

Harnack had inherited his quest for primitive purity from Schleiermacher for whom the essence of any religion is not other than a feeling of dependence. By breaking with Harnack, Barth attains to a position closer to Newman on the implausibility, even more than the futility, of "essence" theology according to Harnack's quixotic expectation. And he considers it an affront, not to the economy of Scripture and Tradition as Newman did, but to the Word of God from which all else springs.[4]

Barth rejects an official system for his dogmatics, not because it would compromise primitive truth, but because a system does not allow for direct obedience to the Word of God. Schleiermacher had not shrunk from a system; he had specifically provided one for locating the Christian essence. Newman certainly had no reservation about a system, though he was not sure what its basis should be. Yet Newman's private awareness of a need to define essentials came about, as did all his science, from an immediate pastoral need, and the need had none of the passion for restoring a simple purity. Newman's early ambition was only to justify the claims of Anglicanism to authentic fullness of doctrine. This had been a motive, of course, in the "Tracts for the Times," and stirred his lengthy correspondence in 1834 with the Abbé Jean-Nicholas Jaegher of the University of Paris, that exchange bearing fruit in the *Lectures on the Prophetical Nature of*

---

[3]John Henry Newman, *Essays Critical and Historical* Vol. II (London: 1872), pp. 233-234.

[4]Cf. Karl Barth, *Church Dogmatics*, ed. G. W. Bromiley and T. F. Torrance (Edinburgh: 1955-), I/2, p. 862, hereafter *Church Dogmatics*: "The Word of God may not be replaced even vicariously by any basic interpretation of the 'essence of Christianity', however pregnant, deep and well-founded."

the Church. The untiring apologetical occupation can be seen in his decision in 1877 to edit and re-issue these lectures under the title, *The Via Media of the Anglican Church*. If hunting for primitive clarity of form is fabulous in the evolution of doctrine, the search for the plenitude of belief is of a real romance. Full Christianity, not simplified Christianity, is the substance of revelation and the working context of Christian life. What Harnack exhibited as simplicity was only static; fullness is organic. But a living organism needs a pattern for development, the gleam of which appears in the *Lectures* to reach high beam in the third edition, the *Via Media*.

In the *Lectures*, Newman pointed to Hooker's fundamental articles which had become rather a litmus for classical Anglicanism: the sacramental system of Baptism and the Eucharist along with the rule of faith of Irenaeus and Tertullian. Still these are signs of the life lived and do not state a basic point behind them, at least as Harnack wanted to quell his fever. If fullness is more to the point than simplification (and the quest for simplicity invariably demands some canon or criterion for simplification), then the essence of fullness lies in whatever structures its unity. Properly understood, as Harnack did not understand it, the essence is constantly "developing" and is not being "restored." And what prevents this development from becoming the baroque degeneration which Harnack detected in all but the most primitive evidences? In answer, Newman could invoke an "idea" over an "essence": "... that development ... is to be considered a corruption which *obscures or prejudices its essential idea*, or which *disturbs the laws of development* which constitute its organization, or which *reverses its course of development*."[5]

Newman broaches the subject to establish a criterion for judging the competing claims or religions according to the

---

[5]John Henry Newman, *An Essay on the Development of Doctrine* (Westminster, Md.: 1968, orig. 1845), 1.3.1., pp. 63f.

standards of change and continuity. His limpid style, not innocent of some syntactical nervousness in theological definitions, calls it "an hypothesis to account for a difficulty"; and that difficulty is one of maintaining in the face of historical trials the principle "that the external continuity of name, profession, and communion, argues a real continuity of doctrine."[6] The Catholic with his structures of authority is obliged, no less than the Protestant, to address the source of the idea behind the doctrine. The question of continuity, a primary one for Newman's whole justification of his conversion, is raised by the third of the three motives which Stephen Sykes has discerned behind the search for essence: it seeks the constitution of legitimacy by which a tradition claims an original or apostolic *imprimatur*.[7] The first motive is simplification (this was Harnack's project, though it is not the private reserve of Liberal Protestantism). St. Augustine's *Enchiridion* is an example as are the Augsburg and Westminster Confessions of the formal Reformed Tradition; the Lambeth Quadrilateral of Anglicanism; and various Catholic manuals and catechisms from the Catechism of the Council of Trent, which Pius XI admired for its elegant Latinity as much as anything else about it, through Cardinal de Gasparri's triple catechism, to a universal catechism for the 1990s. The second motive of the essentialist search is the creation of priorities, one instance of which is the hierarchy of truths spoken of in the Second Vatican Council's Decree on Ecumenism in terms of the *quo* (the authority which gives doctrine its legitimacy) and the *quod* (the content of the doctrine). Barth was inspired and nearly overwhelmed by this creation, or rather assertion, of priorities when he insisted on placing theology under the authority of the Word of God as Christology. The third motive addresses the problem of continuity, establishing apostolic authority; in contemporary

---

[6]Ibid., pp. 53, 33.
[7]Stephen Sykes, *The Identity of Christianity* (London: 1984), pp. 220ff, hereafter *Sykes*.

idiom it obtains principally in the discussion of the development of doctrine. Newman was neither the first nor last moved by this to assert the superior definition of Catholicism over other professions in its economy of developed teaching.

Harnack

As we saw in an earlier chapter, two images regularly occur to Harnack. The more frequent is the one of separating the kernel from the husk. The other, possibly more suited to his purpose in the account of essence, is the sap and bark of a tree. "... the most inward of all possessions, namely, religion does not struggle up into life free and isolated, but grows, so to speak, clothed in bark and cannot grow without it."[8] The essence of Christianity is not to be found solely by examining the original teaching of Jesus, freed from cultural and philosophical accumulations; authenticity is discerned by discovering the source of its vitality. Whether Harnack in fact achieved this is another matter, and one which we have treated, and the case had been made that he imposed his own complex set of assumptions; but he cannot justly be said to discount the function of addenda in religious experience altogether.[9] However, it still is true that searching with Harnack for the authentic Christ is like looking for a fly in amber, and not for a living life. As Catholics collect relics of saints, Harnack collected relics of their faith. Again, what Harnack sought is poorly served if it is seen as nothing more than a reduction to dutiful morality in neo-Kantian guise; but the Kingdom of God is certainly an ethical ideal for Harnack, conspicuous in its contrast to the suprapersonal God of the Idealist, and the "Wholly Other" of Karl Barth. The historical

---

[8]Adolf Harnack, *What is Christianity?* (London: 1901), p. 191, hereafter *WIC*.

[9]Vid. *Sykes*, p. 136.

Jesus, so ardently sought by Harnack, disappears in his own ethicism. Even the Christ of the Synoptics is called into question. The image of Harnack as a child peeling an onion to find the core is valid. And what he claims to find is at least as subjective and elusive as what he meant to discard.

In effect, he managed to radicalize the rejection of metaphysics and the emphasis on morality which Ritschl had shared with the Kantians: "I, too, recognize the mysteries of religious life, but when anything is and remains a mystery, I say nothing about it."[10]   Unlike the apophaticism of the Greek Fathers, what Harnack does not understand of a mystery occasions neglect rather than worship.   John Macquarrie is intrigued by this combination of romanticism and scepticism as Harnack turns it into something of a professional discipline.[11] The mix was rendered bankrupt by the "history of religion" (Religionsgeschichtliche) school which recognized the integrity of the theological questions approached historically.[12] Nor could Harnack's buoyant optimism, never the equivalent of theological hope, withstand the realities of the age; the "essence of Christianity" soon became a hollow corridor in which faintly echoed his once-ringing challenge to "affirm the forces and the standards which on the summits of our inner life shine out as our highest good."[13]

There was nothing for Harnack to fall back on. He had rejected dogma out of hand as an invalid hybrid of religion and metaphysics. The antimetaphysical bias had the stamp of the new modern man about it, the evolution of a bias propagated by Kant whom Gilson called the real father of modern philosophy. Descartes still had managed to assume a scholastic reference,

---

[10]Albrecht Ritschl, *Die christliche Lehre von der Rechfertigung und Versöhnung*, Vol. I (Berlin: 1870), p. 607.

[11]John Macquarrie, *Twentieth Century Religious Thought* (London: 1981), p. 76.

[12]Ibid., p. 139.

[13]*WIC*, p. 301.

however objectively unaware he may have been about it; not so with Kant. Thus Harnack's historical method really went back to nothing, but it did introduce a very modern complex to the concept of original essence.[14] Even Barth's rebellion against Liberalism was so imbued with this prejudice that his reaction against the Kantian disjunction of faith and reason did not revive metaphysics; he behaved in a way ironically attuned to Kantian suspicions when he turned to revelation as the inclusive reference for essentials. To say that revelation is all that counts is nearly twin to saying that all that is known is what is not revelation.

Although Liberal Protestantism received what inspiration it had from the modern air, it was functionally incapable of a remedy for the thoroughly modern anxiety which its neglect of certitude had helped to condition. And it had not found the essence of Christianity. The onion was gone and nothing remained. After all, if it is wrong to put "a christological creed in the forefront of the Gospel . . . ,"[15] and if Christ is distinguished only as the prototype of filial piety, how does he differ from Abraham our father in faith and the whole cloud of witnesses? (cf. Heb. 11) Harnack only replies with a most blatant version of Marcionism, and Marcion thought he was paring the Gospel down to the essence of Christianity, too:

> The rejection of the Old Testament in the second century was an error which the great church rightly opposed; holding on to it in the sixteenth century was a destiny which the Reformation was not able to escape; but for Protestantism to preserve it since the nineteenth century as a canonical document is the result of a religious and ecclesiastical paralysis . . . To clear the table and to honor the truth in our confession and instruction, that is the great feat required of Protestantism today — almost too late.[16]

---

[14]Cf. Macquarrie, op. cit., p. 286.

[15]*WIC*, p. 147.

[16]In Hans Joachim Kraus, *Geschichte der historisch-kritischen Erforschüng des Alten Testaments von der Reformation bis zur Gegenwart*

Thus the essence has become so cerebral that it can dispense with its own historical milieu. But Newman insisted, with that ability to perceive facts which are almost obscured by their very obviousness, that an historical religion contradicts itself when it denies its own saga.

> She began in Chaldea, and then sojourned among the Canaanites, and went down into Egypt, and thence passed into Arabia, till she rested in her own land. Next she encountered the merchants of Tyre, and the wisdom of the East country, and the luxury of Sheba. Then she was carried away to Babylon, and wandered to the schools of Greece. And wherever she went, in trouble or in triumph, still she was a living spirit, the mind and voice of the Most High; "sitting in the midst of the doctors, both hearing them and asking them questions"; claiming to herself what they said rightly, correcting their errors, supplying their defects, completing their beginnings, explaining their surmises, and thus gradually by means of them enlarging the range and refining the sense of her own teaching. So far then from her creed being of doubtful credit because it resembles foreign theologies, we even hold that one special way in which Providence has imparted divine knowledge to us has been by enabling her to draw and collect it together out of the world, and, in this sense, as in others, to "suck the milk of the Gentiles and to suck the breast of kings."[17]

Barth and Harnack

In 1967, Barth said that he hoped very much to come to an agreement with Harnack in heaven. That would have required more of a concession from Harnack, as he had already made evident in their bitter parting of ways in a famous exchange of 1923. That correspondence, and Newman's happier

---

(Neukirchen: 1956), p. 351; quoted in Carl Braaten, *History and Hermeneutics* Vol. II (London: 1968), p. 106.

[17]Newman, *Essays Critical and Historical*, op. cit., p. 232.

correspondence with the Abbé Jaegher, provide monumental specimens of theories working themselves out; the one of 1923 reached an impasse and that of 1834 laid the ground for accord. Barth judged Harnack's essentialism, and indeed any essentialist quest, to be inherently reductionist and counterfeit. And that would be true if essentialism confines itself to uncovering original articles of belief; but such had not been the purpose of essentialism according to Schleiermacher who, if Sykes is correct, in some ways approaches Newman's developmental "idea" theory. In this view, when compared with the sophisticated analyses of both Schleiermacher and Newman, Harnack is an amateur in the scientific comparison of primitive and contemporary Christian systems.[18] Schleiermacher and Newman had maintained an integrity of agreement between primitive experience and developed doctrine. One might even suggest that they were the offended parties, parodied in the radicalizations of their theses respectively by Harnack who abused essence theory and by Loisy who abused development theory.

To Barth, historical consciousness itself was a thing problematic and even alien. He found no relief in anything remotely like Newman's development, or "idea," theory when he rebelled against the static primitivism of Harnack whose quest for the historical Jesus he called a chase after ghosts.[19] He managed to propose an equally static dialectical theory of his own manufacture, professedly obliged to Calvin's Christological axiom, *finitum non capax infiniti*. This he revised later in less philosophical and more Biblical diction as *homo peccator non capax iustitiae Dei*.[20] Revelation thus appears tangential to history, and very different from this persistence of Newman:

---

[18]*Sykes*, pp. 4, 124.

[19]*Church Dogmatics* I/2, pp. 64-65.

[20]Vid. Karl Barth, *Fragments Grave and Gay*, ed. Martin Rumscheidt (London: 1971), p. 15. Cf. Louis Bouyer, *Du Protestantism a L'Église*, p. 52, in Eric Mascall, *Via Media* (London: 1952), p. 142.

... we may determine prayer to be part of Natural Religion, from such instance of the usage as are supplied by the priests of Baal and by dancing Dervishes, without therefore including in our notions of prayer the frantic excesses of the one, or the artistic spinning of the other, or sanctioning their respective objects of belief, Baal or Mahomet.

As prayer is the voice of man to God, so Revelation is the voice of God to man. Accordingly, it is another alleviation of the darkness and distress which weigh upon the religions of the world, that in one way or other such religions are founded on some idea of express revelation, coming from the unseen agents whose anger they deprecate; nay, that the very rites and observances, by which they hope to gain the favour of these beings, are by these beings themselves communicated and appointed. The Religion of Nature is not a deduction or reason, or the joint, voluntary manifesto of a multitude meeting together and pledging themselves to each other, as men move resolutions nor for some political or social purpose, but it is a tradition or an interposition vouchsafed to a people from above. To such an interposition men even ascribed their civil polity or citizenship, which did not originate in any plebiscite, but in *dii minores* or heroes, was inaugurated with portents or palladia, and protected and prospered by oracles and auguries. Here is an evidence, too, how congenial the notion of a revelation is to the human mind, so that the expectation of it may truly be considered an integral part of natural Religion.[21]

Now it would be hard to imagine analogies more unwelcome in the diction of Barth. Things finite are indeed susceptible to the infinite, and nature provides historical clues by which natural religion might accede to revealed truths. Newman is too earthy for Barth, and for that reason Newman can more instinctively take the measure of heaven from his locus on earth, and may even spot a heavenly essence on earth more precisely. The Cardinal would have appreciated the suggestion of Sir Edwyn Hoskyns, that theologians who tend to abstractions and arcane

---

[21]John Henry Newman, *An Essay in Aid of a Grammar of Assent* (Westminster, Md.: 1973, orig. 1870), pp. 92-93, hereafter *Grammar*.

configurations would get a better grip on salvation history if they tried to sacrifice a bull on a hot summer's day.

Natural theology is an insult to grace, in Barth's estimation. There can be no point of contact between creation and creator. For Newman, man had lost his divine likeness (*homoiosis, similitudo*); for Barth, even more than for Luther, the image (*eikon, imago*) itself had been lost. The *analogia entis*, the idea that creatures are capable in and through their creatureliness, of manifesting and understanding God, is rejected by Barth in favor of an *analogia fidei* pure and simple. This is an absolute metaphysical insistence, not simply moral as Brunner made it when he attributed the inadequacy of human reason to human sinfulness. Barth actually thought this signalled a general sketchiness in Brunner's criticism of natural theology. His insistence is direct and relentless: "If we do know about God as the creator, it is neither wholly nor partially because we have a prior knowledge of something which resembles creation. It is only because it has been given to us by God's revelation to know him, and what we previously thought we knew about originators and causes is called in question, turned around, and transformed."[22]   Which moved Macquarrie to respond as Newman probably would have in his own way: "Barth may well be correct in claiming that divine personality, divine fatherhood, and the like, are *ontological* first, and their human analogues derivative; but must not the human analogues be first *epistemological*?"[23]

What intrigued Newman from the anthropological evidence of history repelled Harnack, but neither could have been guilty of making history secede to revelation as though they were hostile. Barth's untempered reaction to the disaster of Liberalism does precisely that and creates a dialectic out of it, using as a proof text: "Though we have known "Christ after the flesh, yet now we

---

[22]Cf. Mascall, op. cit., p. 37; *Church Dogmatics*, I, p. 21.

[23]Macquarrie, op. cit., p. 324.

know him thus no more." (2 Cor. 5:16) It became the theme for a whole procession of dialecticians: Brunner, Gogarten, Bultmann, and Tillich.[24] As Harnack made dogmatics yield to history, so Barth moved dogmatics to the center of the stage; only Newman maintained a balanced economy. For Barth, dogma is not the Word of God revealed in history. It is history's response to revelation. As response, it can hardly claim the social authority which the Church must invoke to reorder and transfigure culture. The naïveté and futility of much social activism by contemporary churchmen influenced by residual Idealist anthropologies and oblivious to a sacramental sense of creation, illustrates this clearly enough. But this is as Barth would have it. If they were together in our imaginary Common Room, Newman should accuse Barth, as Niebuhr did in fact, of "transcendental irresponsibility."[25]   And Harnack would nod assent, if for a wholly different reason.

"The task of theology," says Harnack, "is one with the tasks of science in general . . ." And Barth replies that it is "one with the task of preaching; it consists in taking up and passing on the word of Christ."[26] Barth does not deny the worth of historical criticism to which Harnack was dedicated, nor did he repudiate the systematic theology by which Newman tried to interpret history. But for Barth these could only be legitimate by way of *praeparatio* for the Word of God: ". . . I always thought of historical criticism as merely a means of attaining freedom in relation to the tradition not, however, as a constituting factor in a new liberal tradition."[27] Newman notwithstanding, Barth can admit no natural theology which leads to revealed theology; and philosophical theology is idolatrous, and the worst kind of

---

[24]Braaten, op. cit., p. 58.

[25]Vid. Macquarrie, op. cit., p. 324.

[26]Karl Barth, *Theologische Fragen und Antworten* (Zurich: 1973), pp. 10ff.

[27]*Revolutionary Theology in the Making: Barth-Thurneysen Correspondence 1914-1925*, tr. James D. Smart (Nashville: 1964), p. 32.

idolatry for being narcissistic. Were the *Development of Doctrine* and the *Grammar of Assent* open books to Barth, he would have had to close them.

The essence of Christianity, if the expression is tolerable in any form for Barth, is the kingly freedom of the Word of God; and its quest is a free science only when it obeys this principle. He thought Anselm had done well to speak of *fides quaerens intellectum*, but philosophy and reason can only cooperate, in exegesis and apologetics for example. They do not constitute, or even direct, theology.[28] To Newman, the juxtaposition of reason against revelation is a forced one. Each is but a different form of God's self-communication, and there should be no bald antipathy between ratiocination and God's disclosure of himself in things essential to Christianity. As Austin Farrer urged in his Bampton Lectures, it should be made clear in speaking of reason and revelation that one means natural reason and supernatural revelation. "We have not to distinguish between God's action and ours, but between two phases of God's action — his supernatural action, and his action by way of nature."[29] Through the study of history and his epistemology of inference, Newman was confident that the mind can reasonably decide what is necessary for Christianity to be true to itself.

In contrast, the Barthian ordering turns the matter around: reasons drawn from the accumulated probabilities of historical and religious experience cannot function in a system for faith. And as religion is a product of both, it is not to be confused with dogmatics. The essence of Christianity is not found, then, through religion, as religion is a human search for salvation and is valid only when it modestly understands itself as a halting response to God's Word. This is a decisive tenet of Barth's 1918 commentary on the Epistle to the Romans, with its display of Christ himself as the essential and total context for theology.

---

[28]Cf. Macquarrie, op. cit., pp. 321-322.
[29]Austin Farrer, *The Glass of Vision* (London: 1948), p. 3.

Harnack's ethical idiom for the Kingdom of God is inadequate; Barth brings to it a breathless eschatological interpretation with all of Schweitzer's comprehensiveness, but for him it is a triumphant reality by which the kerygma truly descends from eternity, independent of rational truth or historical experience. If such Christianity exhausts theology, kerygmatic theology exhausts the essence of Christianity in a total contradiction of Harnack's moralizing.

Barth's majestic vertical focus, for all its splendor, is still not more like Newman for being unlike Harnack. The parousia, the second coming, the last judgment and resurrection of the dead are not synchronized to real, or linear, events. They become dimensions of the eschatological approach or revelation to men. Harnack's sentimentalized cameo Christ is shattered by this brilliant spectacle of the "Wholly Other"; yet one looks in vain for the human and cultural focus which Newman provides through the mystery of the Church. Without this historical obedience, the Barthian theology becomes existential in a way which Bultmann eventually would make synonymous with modern egocentrism. And thus we notice the curious affinity between the self-conscious modern outlook and the anti-rationalist tradition which goes all the way back to Schleiermacher's rebellion against Scholasticism and the Enlightenment alike.[30]

Barth modified his position in later years. The revelation which had been understood exclusively as belonging to primal history (*Urgeschicht*) became integrated more to traditional salvation history (*Heilsgeschicht*). But a few short years before his death he still managed to say:

> The kingdom of God is an all-embracing idea. I should say
> that the Church proclaims the kingdom of God (i.e. Jesus
> Christ, who came and will come again, that is, Jesus Christ
> as the Kyrios), and hence God's righteousness (in the

---

[30]Cf. Braaten, op. cit., p. 24.

> biblical sense of the term, in that he works righteousness, the righteousness of his love). And only there should I go on to mention God's commandment. In other words, I should begin with the eschatological idea of the kingdom of God and then state its practical content, God's righteousness in the forgiveness of sins. That is the purport of the Old and New Testaments: the *dikaiosyne theou* (the righteousness of God) and not some other kind of "justice."[31]

He raises the subject as a gloss on the social expression of Pope John XXIII whose concept of the common good he approves, but which risks a glib identification of the Kingdom with its humanitarian application. Even when Barth denounces the way liberal Protestantism isolated Christ's teaching (*evangelium Christi*) from Christ's teaching about himself (*evangelium de Christo*), it is not clear whether he has forsaken facts for abstractions himself. There is a dualist tension in his Christianity no less than in that of Harnack. At least it is hard to expect what construction other than a docetic one can be put on his own claim that "the resurrection of Christ, or his second coming, which is the same thing, is not a historical event."[32] The flat statement has grave consequences if the essential primitive formula, "Jesus is Lord" is a resurrection acclamation. Are we dealing with anything less subjective in Barth than in Harnack? For Harnack's subjectivism comes by de-historicization; Barth's from supra-historicization. Both should pause at Wolfhart Pannenberg's dictum: kerygma without history is meaningless noise.[33] The Kantian subjectivism glares in Barth's radical separation of God and natural history, and in his notion of the readiness of the Holy Spirit to act without relevance to nature;

---

[31]Letter of 15 July 1963, in *Fragments Grave and Gay*, op. cit., p. 80.

[32]Karl Barth, *The Word of God and the Word of Man*, tr. Douglas Horton (New York: 1957), p. 90.

[33]Wolfhart Pannenberg, "Redemptive Event and History" in *Essays on Old Testament Hermeneutics*, ed. Claus Westermann, tr. James Luther Mays (Nashville: 1964), pp. 314-315.

though Barth would have blanched at the suggestion, his version of the Word of God is not always easy to distinguish from the categorical imperative.

While there is a supreme difference between Harnack's essence of Christianity as the simple teaching of Christ, and Barth's essence in terms of Christ himself, there is a parallelism in how they designate the essential tenets. For Harnack, the human Christ, as *Predigt*, has three messages. For Barth, the supernatural Word of God which is Christ is a transcendent proclamation (*Verkundigung*), and it too has three messages. What is essential for Barth becomes a transcendent commentary on the three messages of Christ's teaching de-mythologized by Harnack. Where the first defined by Harnack is the Kingdom of God and its coming, for Barth it is the Word Incarnate by whom the Kingdom comes. Where the second for Harnack is the Fatherhood of God and the infinite value of the human soul, for Barth it is the Holy Scriptures which declare this value. Where the third for Harnack is the higher righteousness and the commandment of love, for Barth it is the proclaimed Word which converts the hearers to this righteousness and commandment by the justification of faith.

Astutely, for he was nothing if not a judge of significant characters, Harnack had detected something in his old student's dialectic which is more than a "naïve biblicism": Barth's is an heuristic boldness which has used biblicism to dignify an "absolute religious scepticism."[34] It certainly is an epistemological scepticism, for Barthian theology has no place for certitude attained rationally. The essence of Christianity is seen by both in ways which could scarcely appear more opposite externally, but opposite in the way sides are opposites of a coin. And the coin in question is the endemic Protestant characterization of grace as extrinsic to the capacity of human

---

[34]Martin Rumscheidt, *Revelation and Theology, an Analysis of the Barth-Harnack Correspondence of 1923* (Cambridge: 1972), pp. 52-53.

nature, and of creation as not only different from, but contrary to, the supernatural order. The issue of Harnack's critique is that grace cannot apply to human nature. According to Barth, grace applies only by ignoring human nature. This does not involve Barth in anything like the reductionism of Harnack; thus Bouyer, not a sympathetic voice by any means, sees "in the giddy sprightliness of (Barth's) glaring nihilism, an apprehension of the sacred greatness of God which has rarely been equalled."[35]

As a common misperception, or to the extent that Harnack and Barth share a view of creation, the fault lies in the decadent kind of late medieval Scholasticism which the Reformation absorbed despite itself. While it also set some of the tone for Counter-Reformation piety and permeated the manuals (there were nominalist professors officially recognized in the Spanish universities of the nineteenth century), it was gradually shunned by Catholicism as it was not shunned by either Liberal or Neo-Reformation Protestantism. Something in the climate is harder to avoid than something in the day's weather. The only Scholastic with whom Luther felt any kinship was Ockham; but Ockham had propounded through nominalism a drastic empiricism which ultimately divested creation of stability, unity, and intelligibility. Examining the coin of grace as Bouyer does, one can mark the head of Barth and the tail of Harnack:

> Never for a moment do we escape from the alternatives. Either a grace which alone saves us, but saves us without touching us, or else a grace which saves us by our independent cooperation, so that strictly speaking we have to save ourselves. Either a faith which is faith in our own faith, that is in our immediate experience and ultimately in that alone, or else a faith which is a pure and simple abdication of ourselves. Either a God who is everything, so that man and the world are literally nothing, or else a world and man which have limited but real powers and values, and then a God who is only the first in a series, a magnified creature but not the creator. Either a Word which remains

---

[35]Louis Bouyer, *Du Protestantisme à l'Église*, op. cit., p. 93.

absolutely foreign to us, which man can only falsify but never interpret and which has no possible meaning for him, or else a word which in the last resort is only his own, in which he himself gives both questions and answers and presumes to attribute to God what is only his own invention.[36]

One practical evidence of the shared nominalism is the anti-sacramental principle at work. Harnack abolishes the sacraments altogether in his essence of Christianity. Barth's position on infant baptism was considered problematic by some of his closest students and, as for Eucharistic theology, he really had none. Though he would later recommend a weekly communion service, he believed it was an escape from grace, a selfish experientialism. If ever Barth becomes uncharacteristically crude and polemical, it is on the matter of Eucharistic doctrine. Through mixed modes, Barth has rejected the sacramental system of sanctifying grace with all the vehemence of Kantian Idealism; Barth because it advertises man's autonomy, Kant because it insults that autonomy! Any system so charged with opposite crimes should either be perverse or perfect. But the only means of intelligibility in a pessimistic creation is, for Barth, the proclamation of the Word of God. "... the scandal of preaching is patently greater than that of 'performing' the miracle of transubstantiation," says Sykes in corroboration of Barth. And that, he says, is only if contemporary miracles are possible in any sense at all.[37]

A Growth That Does Not Outgrow Itself

Newman's Christian "idea" can begin to be grasped once we recognize his basic disagreement with Barth on the dichotomy of Word and Sacrament. There is no test of choice for Newman,

---

[36]Ibid., p. 166. Cf. Mascall, *Via Media*, op. cit., pp. 142ff.
[37]*Sykes*, p. 187.

nor is there even a tension between the two. The Eucharist as the central Christian act manifests the Word and Sacrament cohesively. Newman was a preacher, after all, and Barth could not have esteemed that office more highly than he. But Newman insisted, as Ott would later in commentary on Barth, that if preaching is dogmatics only, then it is "preaching to preachers." Preaching is also hermeneutics in the interest of faith, and the sacraments themselves become a form of preaching by their hermeneutical function. Of course Newman shared with Barth four doctrines which constitute an essence of belief for the Catholic as much as for the Protestant: the gratuitousness of salvation, God's absolute sovereignty, justification by faith, and the divine inspiration of Scripture. By considering them outside the unifying reference of the Church's sacramental life, Barth renders an essence which distorts and exaggerates the developmental idea of Christianity. Newman's critique of the moral to be learned from Protestantism becomes something of a surrogate commentary on what he might have replied to Barth, and even more graphically to Harnack:

> Luther found in the Church great moral corruptions countenanced by its highest authorities; but instead of meeting them with divine weapons, he used one of his own. He adopted a doctrine original, specious, fascinating, persuasive, powerful against Rome, and wonderfully adapted, as if prophetically, to the genius of the times which were to follow. He found Christians in bondage to their works and observances; he released them by his doctrine of faith; and he left them in bondage to their feelings. He weaned them from seeking assurance of salvation in standing ordinances, at the cost of teaching them that a personal consciousness of it was promised to every one who believed. For outward signs of grace he substituted inward; for reverence towards the Church, contemplation of self. And thus, whereas he himself held the proper efficacy of the Sacraments, he has led others to disbelieve it; whereas he preached against reliance on self, he introduced it in a more subtle shape; whereas he professed to make the written

word all in all, he sacrificed it in its length and breadth to the doctrine which he had wrested from a few texts.

This is what comes of fighting God's battles in our own way, of extending truths beyond their measure, of anxiety after a teaching more compact, clear and spiritual, than the Creed of the Apostles. Thus the Pharisees were more careful of their Law than God who gave it; thus Saul saved the cattle he was bid destroy, "to sacrifice to the Lord"; thus Judas was concerned at the waste of the ointment, which might have been given to the poor. In these cases bad men professed to be more zealous for God's honour, more devotional, or more charitable, than the servants of God; and in a parallel way Protestants would be more spiritual. Let us be sure things are going wrong with us, when we see doctrines more clearly, and carry them out more boldly, than they are taught us in Revelation."[38]

The criticism is sounded in Braaten, and almost gloated over by Harnack, of Barth's failure to "go back to the Bible." By way of the Kantian-Ritschlian categorization of reason and revelation, the essence of Christianity for the Barthian is really the confirmation of modern anthropocentrism as it isolates man from knowledge of God. The essence consists in the message which Christ discloses, which is different from the reconciliation he effects in history. The language of the later Barth in the *Church Dogmatics* would modify this starkness; but as Newman indicted Luther, so Barth is indictable for inflating revelation until the historical drama of Christ, climaxing in the eucharistic life of the Church, succumbs to "the hypersensitive epistemological consciousness of modern theology."[39]

Newman was an epistemologist intent on addressing this modern disorientation, and he succeeded to the extent that he was not disorientated by it himself. For the sake of right direction he tried to assimilate the neo-Platonic inwardness, traditional of Augustine and Gregory of Nyssa, with his theory of

---

[38]John Henry Newman, *Lectures on the Doctrine of Justification*, Sixth ed. (London: 1892), pp. 339-341.

[39]Braaten, op. cit., p. 16.

development. Thus, the *Grammar of Assent* and *Development of Doctrine* are books to be read together. But if Barth could have no satisfaction in such reading, he would surely agree with Newman, and indeed says so ever more vociferously, that the theologian is under constant obedience to divine revelation in all its formulations. The Holy Spirit is as central to them as he is neglected by Harnack; in their 1923 correspondence, Harnack mentions him only once, and that in quoting Barth. So we should not be confused to hear from Barth a warning as solemn as that in Newman's "Biglietto Address" with its account of the strange new darkness, worse than the older rationalism, let loose by Liberal optimism and cultural Protestantism. He speaks first of the older, clinical, and defensive atheism of the West "based on the alleged sole validity of the scientific and technological method of thought." This he contrasts with the aggressive political atheism of dialectical materialism in Eastern Europe. Both have their strengths and weaknesses and pathos. But there is another atheism, and this is as virulent as the Liberalism which Newman spent his life exposing:

> The atheism that is the real enemy is the "Christianity that professes faith in God very much as a matter of course, perhaps with great emphasis, and perhaps with righteous indignation at atheism wild or mild, while in its practical thinking and behaviour it carries on exactly as if there were no God. It professes its belief in him, lauds and praises him, while in practice he is the last of the things it thinks about, takes seriously, fears or loves. God is thus turned into an item in the inventory in the contents of an old-fashioned or partially modernized house, a piece of furniture the owner would refuse to part with in any circumstance, but for which he has nevertheless ceased to have any real use; or rather, which he has very good reasons for taking care not to use, for it might be uncomfortable or dangerous. God is spoken of, but what is meant is an idol that one treats as one sees fit. Who can acquit himself of this third form of atheism?[40]

[40]Reply to Max Bense, 14 June 1963, in Karl Barth, *Fragments Grave and Gay*, op. cit., pp. 46-47.

Here, then, is the Christian gentleman of Newman's satire, who is a gentleman but not a Christian. Barth was severe in his judgment: a "dogma, tenet, principle or definition of the essence of Christianity" will not be an adequate refutation of pseudo-Christianity.[41]   Newman was as unequivocal, though his sacralized system would not satisfy Barth as an alternative to the secularizing apostasy of Liberal Protestantism.   Critics have inquired whether Barth's plan of a dogmatics, which interprets events for the Church independently of any system, is less conceptual than the fixed disciplines he rejects. Nonetheless, he shares Newman's distaste for boiling doctrines down to some anticipated essence, even when there is Patristic precedent for valid efforts along this line, such as Irenaeus's summarization of Logos doctrine in his theory of recapitulation.[42]

The four traditional marks of the Church themselves (unity, holiness, catholicity, apostolicity) are not essences but evidences. The same may be said of the three ministerial offices of Christ and the Church; and so Newman subsumes these under theology, since theology "is commensurate with revelation, and revelation is the initial and essential idea of Christianity."[43] Harnack would call that statement extremist metaphysical realism.   In reply, Newman and Barth would declare all Liberal simplification arbitrary. And arbitrariness is neither the ground of unity nor the standard of essentials. Then Newman, quite gently, would of course say the same of Barth's supra-historical revelation.

The attempt to construct a simple essence of Christianity, so characteristic of modern sentimentality, neglects a unifying

---

[41]*Church Dogmatics*, I/2, p. 866.

[42]Ignatius of Antioch (Ep. ad Magnes., 10) had spoken of "Christianismos," or the manner of the true Christian life. This concept of an essence has a long history which approximates a system in Schleiermacher's principle of cohesion, the "Anziehungsprinzip" which he hoped might unite what is common to Protestantism and Catholicism; cf. *Sykes*, p. 215.

[43]Vid. John Henry Newman, *The Via Media of the Anglican Church* Vol. I (London: 1901, orig. 1837), p. xlvii.

matrix for all the ages of Christian experience. But any matrix is incomplete anyway if it presents doctrine without an epistemology to account for assent to that doctrine. Then, as writers like Sykes have gone to lengths to show, systematic and biblical criticism both figure into the discussion of how to resolve the power conflicts arising in any such attempt to identify a unifying principle. Conflict does not disprove the fact of an essential element in Christianity; it only indicates a concept of authority politically as an external regulation and not as a charism of order. Ultimately the distortion is obliged to a notion of the Church's ministry as exclusively didactic rather than hieratic.

Karl Adam reminded his students that while the life of Catholicism grows, it does not outgrow itself.[44] Harnack meant much the same in his image of the sap and bark of a tree, though his practical guide was more his reductionist image of the kernel and husk. Newman and Barth locate the unifying principle of true growth in justification through the cross of Christ. The difference is that Barth expresses this as the manifest Word of God so that the only office in the Church is that of teacher, while Newman speaks of an "idea," not a vague intention or aspiration nor even as the "sacred impression" in his system of assent, but a highly specific dynamic which manifests the Word of God fundamentally in the hieratic constitution of the Church and centrally in the eschatological dimension of the Eucharist.

Barthian essentialism makes history peripheral to dogma. Newman, quite the opposite, finds the essence in history; indeed, the essence of Christianity and the essence of history are inseparable. Newman, then, can confidently say, in the most radical challenge to modern contempt for the spiritual meaning of history, that the "idea" of Christianity is the dynamic, or developmental, union of dogma and time, the animation of the content of revelation by the Holy Spirit who appeals to historical

---

[44]Karl Adam, *The Spirit of Catholicism*, op. cit., p. 150.

reason. This is the doctrine of the First Vatican Council. And, contrary to popular impressions, it is also the appeal of Pius X's *Pascendi* against the Modernists; for its anathemas negated Positivism and Idealism alike, to posit the strength of reason over against the scepticism which tends to issue from Positivism and the solipsism which becomes the fate of Idealism.

There is, then, such a thing as an essence of Christianity in the midst of the controversy about it. But it is not simply Christianity made simple; it cannot be Christ reduced to a few tenets about Christ. The essence of Christianity is not a core but a circumference encompassing the fullness, and this fullness is neither a method capable of being abstracted nor a measure capable of being simplified. Or Newman could appropriate St. Bonaventure to say that the definition is in the power of God whose circumference is nowhere, to focus the ubiquity of his center on one aspect of creation, namely human history. The essence is the dynamic by which the truth of Christ subsists "self-balanced on its center hung" in the Church.[45] The Church can then profess to "Always bearing about in our body the mortification of Jesus, that the life also of Jesus may be made manifest in our bodies." (2 Cor. 4:10)[46] It is therefore of the essence that God's own essence is united to human nature in Christ and is continued in the Church instrumentally and physically.[47]

By their natures, the mystery of Christ and the mystery of human reason approaching Christ do not lend themselves to agreement between the representative figures of Newman and Harnack and Barth. However different their methods, each lived expensively the virtue of freedom. And in the conversation

---

[45]John Henry Newman, *Fifteen Sermons Preached Before the University of Oxford* (London: 1871, orig. 1843), p. 312.

[46]Cf. Newman, *The Via Media of the Anglican Church* Vol. I, op. cit., pp. 354-355.

[47]Cf. eg., St. Thomas Aquinas, *Comm. in Ep. ad Cor.*, 12; *De Veritate*, q. 29, 9.4, ad. 6.

between them as we have imagined it, there have been some sharp things to say. Now each lets the listeners decide for themselves. Meanwhile, Harnack returns to leaf through some history books. Barth reads with deep reverence from his one Book. Newman salutes them both and leaves the Common Room to celebrate Mass.

1983

A Study of Ten Poets

▼▼▼▼▼▼▼▼▼▼▼▼▼▼▼▼▼▼▼▼▼▼▼▼▼▼▼▼▼

Understanding African Poetry

K. L. GOODWIN
Professor, Department of English
University of Queensland

LONDON
HEINEMANN
IBADAN   NAIROBI

Heinemann Educational Books Ltd
22 Bedford Square, London WC1B 3HH
PMB 5205, Ibadan · PO Box 45314, Nairobi

EDINBURGH   MELBOURNE   AUCKLAND
HONG KONG   SINGAPORE   KUALA LUMPUR
NEW DELHI   KINGSTON   PORT OF SPAIN

Heinemann Educational Books Inc.
4 Front Street, Exeter, New Hampshire 03833, USA

ISBN 0 435 91325 5 (cased)
0 435 91326 3 (paper)

Set in 10 pt Plantin
Printed in Great Britain by
Butler & Tanner Ltd, Frome and London